Last Wishes101

DISCOVER PEACE OF MIND

THIS BOOK IS A GUIDE TO THE LAST WISHES OF:

____

NAME

This comprehensive guide to end-of-life planning includes legal forms, estate planning, wills, funeral arrangements, death certificates, obituaries, life insurance, and everything else you need to prepare before you go.

It is suggested that the DNR forms, Pages 11-12 be filled out, copied, and put in a prominent place such as on the refrigerator door.

ISBN-13: 979-8-218-57879-4

Legal and Medical Advice : For legal advice please contact your attorney. For financial advice please contact your accountant. For medical advice please contact your physician

PLEASE NOTE:

This Guide emphasizes forms used in Arizona for Estate Planning. However, most of these forms are generic in nature and are applicable in all States.

This guide can be purchased as a PDF in which the forms can be typed onto and printed. See www.LastWishes101.com

Use of this publication is at your own risk.

This publication does not dispense medical advice or the use of any technique as a form of treatment for physical, emotional, or medical problems without the advice of a personal professional physician, either directly or indirectly. Additionally, this Kit does not dispense legal advice or make any legal or financial recommendation without the advice of professional legal and financial guidance, either directly or indirectly. The intent of the book is only to offer general documentation to help you collect and organize your personal information. Last Wishes 101 LLC and its associates assume no responsibility for your actions in the event you use any information herein for yourself.

Among the many sources referenced for information, we acknowledge Wikipedia, the Social Security Administration, the Veterans Administration, the National Funeral Directors Association, The Wall Street Journal, and many others.

Media and Copyright

Last Wishes101
DISCOVER PEACE OF MIND

Preface:

When I reached 85 years of age I decided I had procrastinated long enough in putting my affairs in order.

I began the arduous task of locating information and legal documents my wife would need upon my passing. I inserted everything I could find about our bank accounts, insurance policies deeds, marriage license, etc. into a three ring note book.

I soon realized there is much more to know about dying than I had ever thought about. Hundreds of hours and pages later I had a somber collection of morbid information. I also found that most material being sold in the market place was at an absurd price and fell short of what most heirs to even a small estate needed.

I have spent a lifetime writing articles and applying for grants. It occurred to me that I could write a book that would help people like me prepare their last wishes, with more information about the subject than presently available. I could also make it interesting and somewhat fun to fill out the forms if I inserted jokes and cartoons concerning death into it. I coined the phrase,
"A lighthearted approach to a serious subject".

I formed an LLC and was joined by Jennifer Sultzaberger as co-author. We put together pertinent forms and topics that most small estates would need, and priced the book with fees about 90% lower than most attorneys charged for less information.

My wife was thrilled with the scrap book and it became the beginning of our book, Last Wishes 101. LastWishes101.Com is our website, and our book can be ordered from Amazon, Barnes and Noble, and your favorite book store. We hope it will be helpful.

(I am not suggesting that you shouldn't use your attorney to examine our Book and help you fill out the forms. We welcome their critique. We offer you an alternative.)

Julian J. Blum

Last Wishes101
DISCOVER PEACE OF MIND

Meet the Authors

ABOUT JULIAN J. BLUM

Overview of his experience and credentials

Author

Julian J. Blum, born in Baltimore, Maryland in 1928, served in the U.S. Navy before relocating to Phoenix, Arizona in 1953. He attended Arizona State University and soon began a distinguished career in real estate. Since 1954, Julian has worked as a licensed Arizona Real Estate Broker, Mortgage Banker, Syndicator, and Developer, with a focus on transformative projects in and around downtown Phoenix.

Julian has also been active in many Civic and Human Service Agencies including: Phoenix JayCees Board, Vice President, Silver Key-Man Award; Jewish Family and Childrens Service, Board President; Central Arizona Shelter Services (CASS) founding Board Member and Vice President; Member Task Force for Homelessness; Lobbyist in Arizona State Legislature for Homeless issues; Valley Forward member of the Board, and member of the Rio Salado Task Force; founder and CEO, New Day Educational Center, a transitional shelter for homeless families now operated as the UMOM New Day Center by the Methodist Outreach Ministries. Julian has written articles and short stories for a variety of local periodicals including Valley Forward, The Real Estate Press, Arizona Human Services Magazine, and The Center City Magazine.

Julian retired from Real Estate brokerage in 2016, and is now devoting his time remembering old friends, making new ones, and supporting the UMOM New Day Center that serves homeless families in need.

ABOUT JENNIFER SULTZABERGER

Overview of her experience and credentials

Author

Jennifer Sultzaberger is a remarkable individual who embodies the qualities of a successful entrepreneur, writer, inventor, and salesperson. With her unique combination of skills and talents, she has been able to make a name for herself in various industries. As a writer, Jennifer has showcased her creativity and storytelling abilities through her captivating works that have resonated with readers worldwide. Her entrepreneurial spirit has allowed her to turn her passion for writing into a thriving business, where she not only writes books but also offers writing services to clients looking to enhance their own projects.

In addition to her writing talents, Jennifer is also a pragmatic thinker, constantly coming up with new and innovative ideas. Her patent held is #vidit. A video SEO marketing platform, combining YouTube and Google search engines, for page one results within the SERP. Jennier used her passion for marketing and the small business owners struggles to compete with the BIGs. This also allows her to provide excellent results for her clients. With her knack for problem-solving and her keen eye for design, Jennifer has proven herself to be a valuable asset in the Digital Marketing industry. Her ability to envision and create new ideas for business growth and measured KPIs sets her apart as a true industry leader.

Moreover, Jennifer's prowess in sales has allowed her to successfully market and sell her guide book to a wide audience. Through her effective communication skills and convincing strategies, she has been able to attract customers and drive sales for her various ventures. Her understanding of consumer behavior and trends has also helped her to adapt her sales techniques to meet the evolving needs of the market. Overall, Jennifer Sultzaberger's multifaceted talents as a writer, entrepreneur, inventor, and salesperson highlight her impressive skills and unwavering dedication to success in the business world.

Last Wishes101

DISCOVER PEACE OF MIND

Contents for Guide: Last Wishes 101

INDEX OF PDF FORMS (For Arizona + your state):

INDEX OF TOPICS:

Last Wishes101
DISCOVER PEACE OF MIND

Last Wishes101
DISCOVER PEACE OF MIND

Instruction

There are numerous ways to optimize your use of this book and make the most of your time. Below is the detailed instructions to assist you at every step of the way:

Hard Copy:
Welcome to your personal organizer! This book is designed to be a practical tool for securely storing important information. We recommend using a pen to fill out the forms for your safety and that of your loved ones.

To accommodate your needs, we've included a usage license allowing you to make photocopies for personal use. This enables you to complete and store the forms in a ring binder or pocket folder alongside this book. Additionally, you'll find Addendum pages at the back for any future updates or changes.

This hard copy is conveniently formatted for easy photocopying, allowing you to reproduce pages by laying them flat on a photocopier as needed.

Digital Copy:

If you have purchased the digital version of this book along with your hardcover copy, you can conveniently enter your information directly into the forms on your computer. Once completed, you have the option to print those forms for your hard copy.

If you haven't yet acquired the digital version but would like to do so, please visit us online at the following website address to obtain your copy lastwishes101.com

The digital version offers enhanced flexibility and ease of use, allowing you to manage your information digitally while maintaining a printed record as well. Thank you for considering the digital supplement to complement your hard copy organizer.

Safe keeping:

For your security, we strongly advise making copies of all documents and storing them in separate locations. This precaution ensures redundancy and safeguards your important information in case of loss or emergency.

Notary Requirements:

Please note that certain documents included in this book necessitate a Notary stamp and signature as a witness. This ensures the authenticity and legal validity of these important records.

Legal Review Advised:

We strongly recommend that you have all documents completed in this book reviewed by your attorney to confirm their validity in your state of residence. Last Wishes 101 LLC and its associates assume no responsibility for any actions taken based on the information provided herein.

Last Wishes101
DISCOVER PEACE OF MIND

In An Emergency Call 911 For: ______________________

(name of the person)

State your name and type of emergency: (i.e. Illness, Death)

Address` ____

Cross-Streets: ____

Describe the problem...

Name: ____________________________ Age: ____________________

Birth Date: ____

Responsible Party: ____

Spouse: ____________________Telephone:______________________

Telephone 2:____

Ambulance Name and Telephone: __________________________

Hospital Preferred: ____________________________________

Social Security #:______________________________________

Hospitalization Insurance Carrier: __________________________

Policy #:____

HMO: ____

I.D. #:____

Primary Physician: ____________________________________.

Telephone #:________________ Religion: ________________

Medicines being taken and other important Information:

____

Preferred Hospice: ____

See the Living Will Documents (attached) located on page: ______________

PREHOSPITAL MEDICAL CARE DIRECTIVE

(DO NOT RESUSCITATE or DNR)

(IMPORTANT – THIS DOCUMENT MUST BE ON PAPER WITH ORANGE BACKGROUND)

MAKE SURE YOU DISPLAY THIS FORM AS VISIBLY AS POSSIBLE FOR FIRST RESPONDERS

GENERAL INFORMATION AND INSTRUCTIONS: A Prehospital Medical Care Directive is a document signed by you and your doctor that informs emergency medical technicians (EMTs) or hospital emergency personnel not to resuscitate you. Sometimes this is called a DNR – Do Not Resuscitate. If you have this form, EMTs and other emergency personnel will not use equipment, drugs, or devices to restart your heart or breathing, but they will not withhold medical interventions that are necessary to provide comfort care or to alleviate pain.

You can either attach a picture to this form OR complete the personal information.

Please take the time to fill out a Health Care Power of Attorney form. That way, if you are unable to communicate your wishes, your agent can sign this form on your behalf, if that is your wish.

This form must be signed by you, in front of your witness or notary. Your Health Care Provider and your witness or notary must also sign this form.

DO NOT have the documents signed by both a witness and a notary, just pick one. If you do not know a notary or cannot pay for one, a witness is legally accepted.

Witnesses or notary public CANNOT be anyone who is:

(a) under the age of 18
(b) related to you by blood, adoption, or marriage
(c) entitled to any part of your estate
(d) appointed as your agent
(e) involved in providing your health care at the time this form is signed

IMPORTANT: Under Arizona law a Prehospital Medical Care Directive or DNR must be on letter sized paper or wallet sized paper on an orange background to be valid.

Office of Arizona Attorney General,
Kris Mayes

PREHOSPITAL MEDICAL CARE DIRECTIVE

In the event of cardiac or respiratory arrest, I refuse any resuscitation measures including cardiac compression, endotracheal intubation and other advanced airway management, artificial ventilation, defibrillation, administration of advanced cardiac life support drugs and related emergency medical procedures.

Patient's Printed Name: ______________________________

Patient's Signature: ______________________________ Date: ______________

***If I am unable to communicate my wishes, and I have designated a Health Care Power of Attorney, my elected Health Care agent shall sign:**

Health Care Power of Attorney Printed Name: ______________________________

Health Care Power of Attorney Signature: ______________________________

PROVIDE THE FOLLOWING INFORMATION OR ATTACH A RECENT PHOTO:

Date of Birth______________

Sex______________

Race______________

Eye Color ______________

Hair Color ______________

INFORMATION ABOUT MY DOCTOR AND HOSPICE (if I am in Hospice):

Physician:______________________________ Telephone: ______________

Hospice Program, if applicable (name):______________________________

SIGNATURE OF DOCTOR OR OTHER HEALTH CARE PROVIDER

I have explained this form and its consequences to the signer and obtained assurance that the signer understands that death may result from any refused care listed above.

Signature of a Licensed Health Care Provider: ______________________________

Date: ______________

SIGNATURE OF WITNESS OR NOTARY (NOT BOTH)

I was present when this form was signed (or marked). The patient then appeared to be of sound mind and free from duress.

Witness Signature:______________________________ Date: ______________

NOTORIAL JURAT:

STATE OF ARIZONA) ss
COUNTY OF ______________)

____

Patient's Name/Health Care Power of Attorney Name

Subscribed and sworn (or affirmed) before me this ______________ day of ______________, 20 ______

Notary Public Signature: ______________________________ My Commission Expires: ______________

Office of Arizona Attorney General,
Kris Mayes

For: ____________________

(name of the person)

Immediate Calls:

Listed below are my most important telephone numbers:

Physicians: ____

____

____

Personal representative (Executor): ______________________________

Funeral Home and Director: ______________________________

Religious Leader: ______________________________

(Bishop, Priest, Pastor, Rabbi, Other)

Employer Name: ____________________ Contact: ____________________

Telephone: ______________________________

Contact the bank and confirm names on signature cards for writing necessary checks (see my assets)

____

Call Attorney: Name: ____________________ Telephone: ______________

Call CPA: Name: ____________________ Telephone: ______________

Location of original Will and trust papers: ______________________________

Others: ______________________________

Last Wishes101

DISCOVER PEACE OF MIND

Please Notify:

For: ______________________________

(name of person)

Listed below are important names and telephone numbers for individuals who should be notified.

Name	Address	Email	Telephone no.

Last Wishes101
DISCOVER PEACE OF MIND

Credit Cards:

For: ______________________
(name of the person)

Send Death Certificates to cancel the cards. Keep full credit card numbers in a safe place.

Card issued by	Address	(Last 4 dig) Card #	Expires	Phone

Mortgage, Auto loan, Lines of credit, etc.

Type of loan	Payable to	Address	Loan Amount	Loan#	Monthly payment

Last Wishes101
DISCOVER PEACE OF MIND

Automatic Bill Payments

For: ____________________
(name of the person)

The following information includes Utility Companies, Retail Stores, Mortgage payments, etc. **Note**: **Password information should be placed with the Executor of your estate prior to your death to be kept in a safe place.**

Monthly payments:

Name	Account #	Product or service	Date Paid	Amount

Last Wishes101
DISCOVER PEACE OF MIND

About my Assets

For: ____________________
(name of person)

My Bank Accounts, Stocks and Bonds, and Real Estate. Print on only one side of the page. **Banks Accounts:**

Contact bank to confirm names on signature cards for writing necessary checks: __________

Remove needed items from safe deposit box at Bank with location of key #______________

authorized person to do so or location of legal papers ____________________________

Name of Bank:	Location:	Account#	Type:
____________	________________	________________	____________
____________	________________	________________	____________
____________	________________	________________	____________
____________	________________	________________	____________

Stocks and Bonds:

Stock Broker ______________________ Account# _________________________

Portfolio:

Stock or Bond:	Symbol:	# of shares:	Original price:	Date of purchase:
__________	__________	__________	__________	__________
__________	__________	__________	__________	__________
__________	__________	__________	__________	__________
__________	__________	__________	__________	__________

Pensions, IRA's, 401 K's, etc: ____

____

____

Real Estate:

Property Location:	Mortgage:	Income:	Other:
____________	____________	____________	____________
____________	____________	____________	____________
____________	____________	____________	____________
____________	____________	____________	____________

Other: ____

____

See file folders located at ____________________________ for additional information.

Last Wishes101

DISCOVER PEACE OF MIND

The page is left blank for additional information and Debts Owed etc...

For ____________________
(name of person)

Tax Information

Print only on the front side of this page. Procedure to follow for gathering tax data:

Personal Income Tax
Location of information for records and of current year:

Location of estimated tax receipts of current year:

Location of records for previous years:

Property Tax
Names of properties owned and taxed:

Name of country to whom taxes are paid:

Addendums, Changes or Additions to pages

For: ____________________
(Name of person)

Feel free to make additional copies of this page.

Additionally, or as a replacement for any content herein, the following should be included:

Last Wishes101
DISCOVER PEACE OF MIND

Funeral Instruction Form

For: ______________
(name of person)

Instructions for administering funeral arrangements. Note: You will need about 20 death certificates.

Name: ______________________ **Telephone:** ______________

Address: ______________________________________

Burial Plot Location: ______________________________

Cremation: ______________________________________

Military Funeral: __________________________________

Memorial Service Details: ____________________________

(Clergy, Other officiating, Location of service)

Emcee: ____

Speakers:

____

____

Casket Preferences: ________________________________

Pall Bearers: ____________________________________

____

Flowers, Donations, etc. ____________________________

Headstone type with inscription as follows: _______________

____

Organ Donation Decisions: ___________________________

Other information: _________________________________

____

____

Last Wishes101

DISCOVER PEACE OF MIND

Personal Data From

For:________________

(name of person)

Name: ____________________________ Telephone: ______________________
E-mail:______________________ Current Address: ______________________

____

Mailing Address: (If different) ____

Place of Birth: ____________________Date of Birth: ____________________

Spouse Name:______________________ Telephone:______________________

E-mail: ___________________ Spouse Address (If different):______________

Date of Marriage: ____________________.

Children's Names, Addresses, Telephone, Grand Children, Pets, or Others:

Mother: ________________________ Father: __________________________

Schools Attended (Names, Degrees, And Professional Designation):

Employer: ______________ Telephone: ____________ Occupation: ________

Occupation: _______________________ Social Security #:_____ _____ _____

Military Service: ___________________ Serial Number: _________________

Dates Served: _________________________ Rank: ______________________

Organization/Memberships: ____

____

Special Achievements, Boards Served: ________________________________

___________________________________ More (See Attached) ___________

Last Wishes101
DISCOVER PEACE OF MIND

Personal Data (Obituary)

For: ______________________
(name of person)

This page is helpful for creating an obituary.

Name: __________________ Telephone:_________________ E-mail:________
Current Address: ____
Mailing Address (if different): _______________________________________
Telephone: _____________ E-mail: _____________________________________
Spouse Name: _____________ Telephone: ______________E-mail: _________
Place of Birth: __________________ Date of Birth: ______________________
Spouse Name: ______________________ Telephone: _____________________
E-mail: ___________ Spouse Address (If different): _____________________
_________________________Date of Marriage: ___________________.
Children's Name, Addresses, Telephone, Grand Children, Pets, or other:

Mother: ________________________ Father: ___________________________
Schools Attended (Names, Degrees, And Professional Designation):

Employer: ______________ Telephone: ____________ Occupation:________
Occupation:_______________________ Social Security #:_____ _____ _____
Military Service: ____________________ Serial Number: _________________
Dates Served: _________________________ Rank:_______________________
Organization/Memberships: ____
____
Special Achievements, Boards Served: ________________________________
___________________________________ More (See Attached) ___________

My Obituary

See attached photo.

For: ____________________
(name of person)

Last Wishes101

DISCOVER PEACE OF MIND

For: ______________________
(name of person)

About My Pets

All necessary information about my pets:

Type of Pet: ______________________ Name: ______________________________________

Age: _____________ Veterinarian:____

Telephone:________________________ Upon my death, if my partner is unable to care for_________________ I do hereby give ________________ to ________________________.

Type of Pet:______________________ Name:______________________________________

Age:_____________ Veterinarian:____

Telephone:________________________ Upon my death, if my partner is unable to care for_________________ I do hereby give ________________ to ________________________.

Type of Pet: _____________________ Name:______________________________________

Age:_____________ Veterinarian:____

Telephone:________________________ Upon my death, if my partner is unable to care for_________________ I do hereby give ________________ to ____.

Type of Pet: ___________________

Name:____ Age:_________________________

Veterinarian:____

Telephone:________________________ Upon my death, if my partner is unable to care for_________________ I do hereby give ________________ to ________________________.

OTHER PETS AND DISPOSITION

____

____

____

____

____

PLEASE ATTACH PAGES FOR ADDITIONAL INFORMATION ABOUT PETS INCLUDING CARE AND FEEDING INSTRUCTIONS

GENERAL POWER OF ATTORNEY

1. CHECK MARK ONE (1) TYPE OF POWER OF ATTORNEY:

☐ **General Regular Power of Attorney (has a beginning and end date), OR**

☐ **General Durable Power of Attorney (ends upon Principal's death or revocation)**

2. IDENTIFY the Principal and Attorney-in-Fact:

	Name	Address of Residence	City	State	Zip Code	Date of Birth
Principal:						
Agent / Attorney-In-Fact:						

3. MARK the Sections that apply to you.

Principal, an individual, hereby appoints the above-named Agent/Attorney-in-Fact to act in name and place of Principal to perform the following general matters.

Scope and extent of powers granted by the General Power of Attorney: to exercise any or all of the following powers concerning:

☐ **a.** Personal Finances: to withdraw and deposit funds from bank accounts belonging to Principal and to enter and remove the contents of all safe deposit boxes rented by the principal; to ask, demand, sue for, recover, collect, and receive each and every sum of money, debt, account, legacy, bequest, interest, dividend, annuity and demand which now is or hereafter shall become due, owing or payable, belonging to or claimed by Principal and to use and take any lawful means for the recovery thereof by legal process or otherwise, and to execute and deliver a satisfaction or release therefor, together with the right and power to compromise or compound any claim or demand; to borrow money and to execute and deliver notes with or without security; and to loan money and receive notes with such security as Attorney-in-Fact shall deem proper;

☐ **b.** Real property, or any interest therein or any improvements thereon: to contract for, purchase, receive and take possession thereof and of evidence and title thereto; to lease the same for any term or purpose, including leases for business residence; to sell, exchange, subdivide, grant or convey the same with or without warranty, covenant or restrictions; to mortgage, transfer in trust, or otherwise encumber the same to secure payment of a note or performance of any obligation or agreement;

☐ **c.** Personal property: to contract for, buy, sell, exchange, transfer, endorse and in any legal manner deal in and with the same; and to mortgage, transfer in trust, or otherwise encumber the same to secure payment of a note of performance of any obligation or agreement;

☐ **d.** Business Transactions of any kind, and as the act and deed of Principal to sign, execute, acknowledge and deliver any deed, lease, assignment of lease, covenant, indemnity, agreement, mortgage, deed of trust, assignment of mortgage, or beneficial interest under deed of trust, subdivision or plat, extension or renewal of any obligation, subordination or waiver of priority, bill of lading, bill of sale, bond, note, receipt, check, evidence of debt, full or partial release of mortgage judgment or other debt, and such other instruments in writing of any kind or class as may be necessary or proper in the premises;

☐ **e.** To do and perform every and all acts required, necessary or appropriate to be done in and about the premises as fully to all intents and purposes as Principal might or could do if personally present, hereby ratifying all that Attorney-in-Fact shall lawfully do or cause to be done by virtue of this General Power of Attorney.

4. CHECK the ONE type of Power of Attorney that applies to you. Complete the information asked for in the Section.

☐ **General Regular Power of Attorney** - Has beginning and ending dates.

- Effective Date: the time from which this document is operational: ____________________, 20______.

  This General Power of Attorney begins on the above effective date and continues until the expiration date of ____________________ 20 ________, unless the Principal revokes this Power of Attorney before expiration using a written document of Revocation.

- Manner of Revocation: The Principal may revoke this document in writing at any time before the expiration date for no reason or for cause. Also, if the Attorney-in-Fact exceeds or violates the scope and authority granted by this document, the Principal may revoke in writing the Power of Attorney at any time before the expiration date.

☐ **General Durable Power of Attorney** – Has a beginning effective date and lasts until the death of the Principal or until revocation.

- Effective Date: the time from which this document is operational: ____________________, 20______.

- Manner of Revocation: The Principal may revoke this document in writing at any time before the expiration date for no reason or for cause, or if the Attorney-in-Fact exceeds or violates the scope and authority granted by this document. *If the Principal becomes disabled or incapacitated, the Attorney-in-Fact may continue acting as such despite the disability, incapacity or the expiration date.*

5. COMPENSATION of Attorney-in-Fact: None.

This portion of page left blank intentionally

6. SIGNATURES.

For Principal:

I, ______________________________, the principal, sign my name to this power of attorney this ____ day of ____________________ and, being first duly sworn, do declare to the undersigned authority that I sign and execute this instrument as my power of attorney and that I sign it willingly, or willingly direct another to sign for me, that I execute it as my free and voluntary act for the purposes expressed in the power of attorney, and that as required by A.R.S. § 14-5501, I am eighteen years of age or older, of sound mind, and under no constraint or undue influence.

____
Principal

For Witness:

I, ______________________________, the witness, sign my name to the foregoing power of attorney being first duly sworn, and do declare to the undersigned authority the principal signs and executes this instrument as the principal's power of attorney and that the principal signs it willingly, or willingly directs another to sign for the principal, and that I, in the presence and hearing of the principal sign this power of attorney as witness to the principal's signing, and to the best of my knowledge the principal is eighteen years of age or older, of sound mind, and under no constraint or undue influence.

____
Witness

7. NOTARIZATION.

STATE OF ____________________________

COUNTY OF __________________________

Subscribed, sworn to or affirmed, and acknowledged before me by ____________________, the principal, and subscribed and sworn to or affirmed before me by ______________________________, witness, this ______ day of ____________.

(notary seal)

____
Notary Public

LIFE CARE PLANNING

Advance Directives for Making Your Health Care Decisions

Provided by

The Office of Arizona Attorney General, Kris Mayes

MAIL FORMS TO:

AZ Healthcare Directives Registry
2901 N. Central Ave. Ste. 1100
Phoenix AZ 85012

OR

Email:

documents@azhdr.org

OR

Fax: 602-264-8823

his packet was last updated 01/2023

WHAT IS LIFE CARE PLANNING AND WHY IS IT SO IMPORTANT?

Life Care Planning is the process of deciding your medical wishes and who you want to carry them out, in case you are unable to do so. The documents in this packet are meant for you to express your wishes, whatever they may be, so you receive the treatment you want if you can no longer communicate. Hopefully, having your wishes clearly stated will help those close to you avoid the pain of trying to guess what you would or would not want done.

Life Care Planning is an important task for all of us, whether young or old, healthy or facing challenges. None of us knows what life has in store, so taking steps to tell our loved ones of our wishes can make all the difference on our end of life care. Through increased awareness and access to information, Arizonans of all ages can make their choices known about who will manage their medical affairs in the event of an emergency.

WHY DOES THE ARIZONA ATTORNEY GENERAL OFFER THESE FORMS?

The Arizona Attorney General's Office wants to make sure that all Arizonans have access to these free legal documents, all of which are in line with Arizona Law. The Attorney General's Office is just one of several places to get forms and information on life care planning. The Attorney General's Office is not recommending any particular choices but does urge you to think about these choices, discuss them with your loved ones, and complete the right documents for your situation.

The primary role of the Attorney General's Office is to provide legal representation to the State of Arizona, its agencies, and State officials acting in their official capacities. The Office cannot give legal advice or represent private citizens on personal legal matters. If you need help with a personal legal matter—such as filing a lawsuit, creating a will, or defending against a criminal charge—you may want to contact a private attorney.

TALKING WITH OTHERS ABOUT YOUR WISHES

You should consider the people that you can begin your life care planning conversations with. Your medical care is about you - start the conversations with those who can help you consider what medical treatments you may or may not want if you become incapacitated, or as you approach the end of your life.

- **Your Health Care Agent (the person you select to make health care decisions for you)**
- **Your Spouse, Children, Other Relatives, and Close Friends**
- **Your Doctor, Clergyperson and Others**

DOCUMENTS INCLUDED IN THIS PACKET

- **Life Care Planning Checklist**
    - This document lists out all the forms in the packet so that you can check off which ones you have completed. If you wish to register your documents with the Arizona Health Care Directives Registry, the checklist will let you know which forms are accepted.

- **Health Care Power of Attorney**
    - This form allows you to select a person to make future medical decisions for you if you become too ill to communicate or cannot make those decisions for yourself.

- **Living Will**
    - This form allows you to list out the type of medical treatments you do or do not want for your end of life care. It should go with your Health Care Power of Attorney form so your agent knows your wishes.

- **Mental Health Care Power of Attorney**
    - This form allows you to select a person to make future mental health care decisions for you in case you become incapable of making those decisions for yourself.

- **Prehospital Medical Care Directives (Do Not Resuscitate)**
    - This form needs to be on orange paper and should be signed by you and your doctor. It informs emergency medical technicians (EMTs) or first responders not to resuscitate you. Sometimes this is called a DNR – Do Not Resuscitate. Please note this is valid prior to going to a hospital, if admitted to a hospital they may require you to fill out another form for their hospital.

- **Registration Agreement**
    - If you would like to register your documents with the Arizona Health Care Directives Registry, you MUST fill out this form and submit it with your documents.

WHAT DOES THE LAW SAY?

If you are interested in the laws written about the forms in this packet you can look them up at www.azleg.gov/arstitle/

- **Health Care Power of Attorney:** Arizona Revised Statutes §§ 36-3221 *et seq.*
- **Health Care Directives:** Arizona Revised Statutes §§ 36-3201 *et seq.*
- **Agents or Surrogate Decision-Makers:** Arizona Revised Statutes §§ 36-3231 *et seq*
- **Living Will:** Arizona Revised Statutes §§ 36-3201 *et seq* AND §§ 36-3261 *et seq.*
- **Mental Health Care Power of Attorney:** Arizona Revised Statutes §§ 36-3201 *et seq* AND §§ 36-3281 *et seq.*
- **Prehospital Medical Care Directives (Do Not Resuscitate):** Arizona Revised Statutes § 36-3251.

WHAT TO DO WITH THESE DOCUMENTS IN 4 STEPS

Step 1: Fill out all forms that apply to you and express your wishes for your end of life care.

Read through the documents carefully to select choices that are best suited to your wishes. Each document will need to be notarized OR witnessed. DO NOT have the documents signed by both, just pick one. If you do not know a notary or cannot pay for one a witness is legally accepted.

Witnesses or Notary Public CANNOT be anyone who is:

(a) under the age of 18

(b) related to you by blood, adoption, or marriage

(c) entitled to any part of your estate

(d) appointed as your agent

(e) involved in providing your health care at the time this form is signed

Step 2: Keep the originals in a safe place that is easily accessible.

It is important to review your documents from time to time. Give copies to the person you choose as your agent, as well as your doctor and anyone else who may be contacted about your wishes, such as family members and close friends. Keep a few extra copies and be sure to take one with you if you go to a hospital or other health care provider.

Step 3: Register your documents on the Arizona Health Care Directives Registry. *(Optional)*

You can mail, email or fax copies of the documents and the registration form to the registry. The information to send the documents to is on the cover of this packet and below.

AZ Healthcare Directives Registry
2901 N. Central Ave. Ste. 1100
Phoenix AZ 85012
OR
Email: documents@azhdr.org OR Fax: 602-264-8823

The purpose of registering Life Care Planning forms is to create a centralized location where your relatives, first responders, a hospital, or other health care facility can access the forms if they are not readily available.

Step 4 – If Needed: Replacing Existing Directives.

To make changes to your existing documents, you will need to complete any forms that are affected by that change, i.e. change of address, wishes, or agent. It is important that you have a list of people with copies of your documents so that you can send them all an updated version if needed or a letter revoking the forms. The state will accept the most recent version of your documents.

If you have registered your documents with the Registry, you will need to fill out another registration form and indicate that you are replacing, adding, or revoking documents in the Registry.

LIFE CARE PLANNING IN OTHER STATES

- If you have advance directives from another state, district, or territory of the US, Arizona Revised Statutes §§ 36-3208 *et seq* says it is *"valid in this state if it was valid in the place where and at the time when it was adopted and only to the extent that it does not conflict with the criminal laws of this state."*
- If you have Arizona advance directives, you will need to check with the Attorney General's Office in the other state to find out if they accept Arizona's documents.

FREQUENTLY ASKED QUESTIONS:

1. **Where can I find these free forms?**
   - You can get copies of this Life Care Planning packet and the individual forms on the Attorney General's website at https://www.azag.gov/seniors/life-care-planning, or by calling the Community Outreach and Education Section at 602-542-2123.

2. **If I do not fill out these forms who will make medical decisions for me?**
   - If you did not leave a Health Care Power of Attorney and there is no court appointed guardian, health care providers will contact the following people, in this order, who will have the authority to make health care decisions for you.
   - These people are called "surrogates."
     1. Your spouse, unless you and your spouse are legally separated.
     2. Your adult child. If there is more than one adult child, the health care providers will seek the consent of a majority of the children who are available for consultation.
     3. Your parent.
     4. Your domestic partner if no other person has assumed any financial responsibility for you.
     5. Your brother or sister.
     6. Your close friend.

3. **Should I complete a Do Not Resuscitate "DNR" Form?**
   - If you are healthy and strong, you may not wish to complete a DNR. You can express your wishes about how you want to be cared for should you become seriously ill without completing a DNR. DNRs are most appropriate for people who would probably not do well with CPR (cardiopulmonary resuscitation) because they are very sick, terminally ill or otherwise extremely weak. In any case, you will need to discuss the DNR with your doctor, who will also need to sign the form.

4. **At what age should I think about filling out these documents?**
   - Now, so long as you are at least 18 years of age. It is never too early to be prepared.

5. **Will I need a lawyer to fill out these forms?**

- No. You do not need a lawyer's help to fill out these documents, but you may wish to consult with a lawyer if you need advice. If you need to find an attorney, you can reach out to these legal services for help:

- **Arizona State Bar**
  - **(602) 252-4804 or** www.azbar.org

  For help finding an attorney in your budget, area, and skill in the type of help needed.

- **24-hour Senior HELP LINE**
  - Within Maricopa County - **(602) 264-HELP / (602) 264-4357**
  - Outside Maricopa County – toll free - **1-888-264-2258**.

  There are Area Agency on Aging regional offices designated to serve each Arizona county. See your local telephone book for the closest regional office or go to www.des.az.gov and search Area Agency on Aging for locations.

- **Elder Law Hotline**
  - **1-800-231-5441**

  Free legal advice, information, and referrals provided o Arizona residents 60 years of age or older, or to family members calling on behalf of a senior. Attorneys do not provide services in criminal matters, and do not represent clients in court proceedings. They give advice, information, and referrals on a wide variety of legal matters important to seniors. Funded by the Arizona Supreme Court and operated by Southern Arizona Legal Aid, Inc.

WALLET-SIZED NOTICE:

Complete and cut out the notice below. Keep it in your wallet with your driver's license and insurance cards so that law enforcement and medical personnel will know who to contact for copies of your advanced directives.

NOTICE IN CASE OF ACCIDENT OR EMERGENCY:
My Name:
Date:

I have signed the following forms: (check)
☐ Health Care Power of Attorney
☐ Living Will
☐ Mental Health Care Power of Attorney
☐ Prehospital Medical Directive (Do Not Resuscitate)

Please contact the following for copies:
Name:
Telephone:

LIFE CARE PLANNING CHECKLIST

- ❑ Registration Agreement
  - This form HAS to be included if you want to register ANY forms.
- ❑ Health Care Power of Attorney
- ❑ Living Will
- ❑ Mental Health Care Power of Attorney
- ❑ Prehospital Medical Care Directive (Do Not Resuscitate)

To register your completed documents, make photo copies and send the copies to:

AZ Healthcare Directives Registry
2901 N. Central Ave. Ste. 1100
Phoenix AZ 85012

OR

Email: documents@azhdr.org

OR

Fax: 602-264-8823

contexture | ARIZONA Healthcare Directives Registry

REGISTRATION AGREEMENT

About this Agreement: The Arizona Department of Health Services (ADHS) has designated Health Current to operate the Arizona Healthcare Directives Registry ("**AzHDR**"). The AzHDR is a **free** registry that provides secure electronic storage and access to advance directives. This registry service is NOT the Health Current health information exchange (HIE).

PLEASE READ THIS DOCUMENT CAREFULLY. This is a legally binding agreement (the "Registration Agreement") between you ("you" or "your") and Health Current ("we" or "us") about your submission of documents to the AzHDR. If the instructions herein are not followed, your form(s) may be rejected.

How to complete this Agreement:

- Read the agreement and complete this form.
- Fill in **all** blank spaces on this form.
- Sign and date form.
- Attach a copy of the witnessed or notarized advance directive(s). DO NOT SEND ORIGINALS TO THE AZHDR.
- Mail to: AzHDR – Health Current
2901 N. Central Ave., Ste. 1100
Phoenix, AZ 85012
- Or fax to: 602-264-8823
- Or email to: documents@azhdr.org

Processing time: up to three weeks.

REQUIRED REGISTRANT INFORMATION

Last Name:	**First Name:**	**Middle Name:**
Address:		**Date of Birth:** MM/DD/YYYY
City:	**State:**	**Zip:**
Phone: ☐ I choose to opt out of SMS text	**Email:** ☐ I choose to opt out of email	
Mailing address if different from above:		
City:	**State:**	**Zip:**

Check the applicable box (check only one box per submission):

☐ New registration.
☐ Replace an advance directive(s) presently in the AzHDR with the new one(s) attached.
  ☐ Replace all documents presently in the registry with the new one(s) attached.
  ☐ Replace only the following document type(s) presently in the registry with the new one(s) attached while leaving the others in place (check all that apply):
    ☐ Living will ☐ Health care power of attorney ☐ Mental health care power of attorney ☐ DNR
☐ Add an additional document to my currently stored directive(s).
☐ Inactivate my account: Check this box if you do not want your documents to be active in the registry.
☐ Change registrant demographic information previously submitted (update your information on this form).

Please note: All documents submitted to Health Current must be copies. Please do not submit originals. Once your account has been activated and your documents have been uploaded to the AzHDR, Health Current will not retain paper copies of your advance directives. Additionally, any documents received by Health Current that are not advance directives or attachments thereto will not be accepted and will be shredded and securely destroyed.

Arizona Advance Directives Registration Agreement Terms & Conditions

1. **The AzHDR.** The AzHDR is a free online registry for securely storing and accessing advance directives electronically. The Arizona Department of Health Services ("ADHS") has designated Health Current to operate the AzHDR. (*see* A.R.S. §§ 36-3291 through 3297). Health Current has contracted with a technology vendor(s) ("Vendor") to power this service. Use of the AzHDR is voluntary. Your decision to submit (or not submit) documents to the AzHDR will **NOT** affect the validity or revocation of any advance directives. While Health Current and its Vendor enable individuals to submit, store and access advance directives, Health Current and its Vendor do not take any part in, and are not responsible for, whether or how these advance directives are used or any interactions between you and third parties.

2. **Submitting Advance Directives.**

(a) Advance Directives. The documents that may be submitted to the AzHDR are limited to health care powers of attorney, mental healthcare powers of attorney, living wills, and prehospital medical care directives, as well as any attachments and any amendments thereto (collectively, "advance directives"). Arizona law requires that documents submitted to the AzHDR be notarized or witnessed. **You must NOT submit any original documents to the AzHDR. Original documents may not be returned. All documents submitted must be copies. Once accessible in the AzHDR, any paper documentation submitted to Health Current will be shredded and securely destroyed. Health Current will not retain paper copies of your advance directives.**

(b) Representation and Warranty. You represent and warrant that the information you provide to us is accurate, current and complete. This is an ongoing representation and warranty. You must not misrepresent your identity, provide false information, impersonate another person, or misrepresent your relationship with a person.

(c) Consent. By submitting documents to the AzHDR, you are giving your permission for Health Current to store these documents and make them accessible to third parties subject to applicable law. You must follow all the laws that apply to you regarding the release of information to the AzHDR. You are solely responsible for obtaining and any all consents or authorizations that you determine are required by the laws that apply to you to release information (including without limitation advance directives) to the AzHDR (collectively, "Consent").

(d) Activation. You acknowledge and agree that in order to activate your submission of an advance directive to the AzHDR, we must receive confirmation that the information submitted is correct. We may ask you for that confirmation. If applicable to your submission, you acknowledge, agree and authorize Health Current to provide your submission and the details surrounding that submission to the person who is the subject of the advance directive. You further authorize us to contact that person using the contact information you have provided to us. For example, if you are submitting an advance directive for another person, and you give us that person's physical address, email address or telephone phone number, you authorize us to use that contact information to inform that person that you have submitted an advance directive about that person.

(e) Identity Verification. Before we activate your document submission(s), we will also require you to verify your identity. In order to do that, you will be required to provide certain personal information about yourself and may be asked to provide personal information about the person who is the subject of the advance directive if you are submitting the advance directive for someone other than yourself. If you submit this Agreement and your advance directive by fax or mail to Health Current, you will be required to have your signature notarized to verify your identity. By signing this agreement before a notary public, you hereby consent to this form of identity verification. You represent and warrant that you have obtained any and all Consents to provide personal information about another person as part of your submission.

(f) No Document Validation. You acknowledge that Health Current has no obligation to pre-screen, verify or validate the advance directive(s) or any other documents you submit to the AzHDR; however, we reserve the right in our sole discretion to pre-screen, refuse to activate, or remove any document if it violates this Registration Agreement or is otherwise objectionable.

3. **Accessing Advance Directives.**

(a) Your AzHDR Account. Once we receive your document submission, we will create an AzHDR account that you can claim by registering with us at signup.azhdr.org You may review, retrieve, revoke and replace documents through your AzHDR account or by contacting us at info@azhdr.org It may take up to three weeks for us to process a request. A revocation or replacement is not effective until it is processed, and it will not affect any access, disclosure, use or other action taken in reliance on a previously submitted document before the effective date of the change.

(b) Security. Health Current uses industry standard safeguards to ensure the security, privacy and integrity of the AzHDR, but we need your help. You must protect your AzHDR account information and credentials. Health Current and its Vendor will not be responsible for any loss or damage caused by someone else using your account.

(c) Privacy. Health Current will not use or disclose information we maintain for the AzHDR except as allowed by state or federal law, including the AzHDR Confidentiality Law (see A.R.S. § 36-3295). Please read the Privacy Policy on the AzHDR website (azhdr.org) to learn how information about you is collected, used, and shared in connection with the AzHDR. By signing this Registration Agreement or by submitting documents to the AzHDR, you are also agreeing to the Privacy Policy. The Privacy Policy (and changes to it) are incorporated by reference into these Terms & Conditions.

(d) DISCLAIMER. HEALTH CURRENT AND ITS VENDOR DO NOT GUARANTEE THAT INFORMATION (INCLUDING WITHOUT LIMITATION ADVANCE DIRECTIVES) ON OR ACCESSIBLE THROUGH THE AZHDR WILL BE ACCURATE, COMPLETE, TIMELY (REAL TIME OR CONTINUOUSLY), ERROR-FREE, SECURE, OR WITHOUT INTERRUPTIONS, OR THAT ANY ERRORS WILL BE CORRECTED. YOU UNDERSTAND AND AGREE THAT THE AZHDR IS PROVIDED "AS IS" AND "AS IS AVAILABLE" WITH ALL FAULTS. NEITHER HEALTH CURRENT NOR VENDOR SHALL BE LIABLE FOR THE LOSS, DESTRUCTION OR UNAVAILABILITY OF ALL OR PART OF YOUR SUBMITTED DOCUMENTS.

4. **Electronic Communications.** By giving us your contact information, you are agreeing to receive communications, including without limitation calls, emails, text messages and notifications, from Health Current, Vendor and/or our affiliates about the document(s) you submitted and/or your use of the AzHDR, including without limitation notices and advisories. These communications may be done by automated dialing equipment and/or artificial voice or prerecorded messages. You may receive multiple messages each day. Standard message and data rates apply. We are not responsible for any data transmission fees. You can opt out at any time from receiving text messages by replying "STOP." This opt-out process does not apply to live phone calls or emails, which may continue in case we need to reach you.

5. **Limitations of Liability.** YOU UNDERSTAND AND AGREE THAT HEALTH CURRENT, ITS MEMBERS, OFFICERS, DIRECTORS, REPRESENTATIVES, EMPLOYEES, AGENTS, AFFILIATES, VENDOR AND BUSINESS PARTNERS (COLLECTIVELY, "HEALTH

CURRENT PERSONNEL"), WILL NOT BE LIABLE TO YOU OR ANYONE ELSE FOR ANY INDIRECT, INCIDENTAL, CONSEQUENTIAL (INCLUDING WITHOUT LIMITATION LOST REVENUES OR LOST PROFITS), PUNITIVE, OR EXEMPLARY DAMAGES, PENALTIES, OR SPECIAL LIABILITY ARISING OUT OF OR IN ANY WAY CONNECTED WITH YOUR DOCUMENT SUBMISSIONS. IN NO EVENT WILL HEALTH CURRENT PERSONNEL'S LIABILTY ARISING OUT OF OR RELATED TO USE OF THE AZHDR EXCEED $50.00. ANY CAUSE OF ACTION OR CLAIM YOU MAY HAVE ARISING OUT OF OR IN ANY WAY CONNECTED TO YOUR DOCUMENT SUBMISSION MUST BE COMMENCED WITHIN ONE (1) YEAR AFTER THE CAUSE OF ACTION ACCRUES, OTHERWISE SUCH CAUSE OF ACTION OR CLAIM IS PERMANENTLY BARRED. YOU ACKNOWLEDGE AND AGREE THAT HEALTH CURRENT PERSONNEL ARE NOT LIABLE, AND YOU AGREE NOT TO SEEK TO HOLD THEM LIABLE, FOR THE CONDUCT OF THIRD PARTIES. THE FOREGOING LIMITATIONS WILL APPLY WHETHER SUCH DAMAGES, LIABILITY, CAUSES OF ACTION OR CLAIMS ARISE OUT OF BREACH OF CONTRACT, TORT (INCLUDING NEGLIGENCE), OR OTHERWISE, AND REGARDLESS OF WHETHER SUCH DAMAGES, LIABILITY, CAUSES OF ACTION OR CLAIMS WERE FORESEEABLE OR HEALTH CURRENT PERSONNEL WERE ADVISED OF THE POSSIBILITY OF SUCH DAMAGES, LIABILITY, CAUSES OF ACTION OR CLAIMS.

6. **Indemnification and Release.** YOU AGREE TO INDEMNIFY, DEFEND AND HOLD HARMLESS HEALTH CURRENT PERSONNEL FROM ANY AND ALL CLAIMS, DEMANDS, ACTIONS OF ANY KIND, LOSSES, EXPENSES, DAMAGES AND COSTS (INCLUDING WITHOUT LIMITATIONS REASONABLE ATTORNEYS' FEES) (COLLECTIVELY, "LOSSES") ARISING OUT OF OR IN ANY WAY CONNECTED WITH YOUR DOCUMENT SUBMISSIONS. You further agree to release Health Current Personnel and their successors from any and all Losses (including without limitation personal injuries and death) arising out of or in any way connected with the actions or omissions of third parties in connection with the AzHDR.

7. **CLASS ACTION AND JURY TRIAL WAIVER.** YOU AGREE THAT DISPUTES BETWEEN YOU AND HEALTH CURRENT OR ITS VENDOR WILL BE RESOLVED IN ACCORDANCE WITH THIS SUBMISSION AGREEMENT AND YOU WAIVE YOUR RIGHT TO PARTICIPATE IN A CLASS OR COLLECTIVE ACTION LAWSUIT, OR CLASS OR COLLECTIVE ARBITRATION. YOU AND HEALTH CURRENT WAIVE ALL RIGHTS TO A JURY TRIAL AND ELECT INSTEAD TO HAVE A JUDGE RESOLVE THE DISPUTE.

8. **Miscellaneous.** If any provision of this Submission Agreement is found to be unenforceable or invalid, such provisions will be deleted without affecting the remaining provisions. Arizona law governs the interpretation of this Registration Agreement, and will apply if there are disputes. Disputes will be settled in Maricopa County, Arizona, and you agree to submit to the exclusive personal jurisdiction of state and federal courts located in Maricopa County, Arizona.

Registrant Attestation (NOTARIZATION REQUIRED)

By signing below, I certify that I have read, understand, and agree to this AzHDR Registration Agreement, including without limitation the Terms and Conditions contained herein. I understand that once a submitted document is activated, it may be accessible to healthcare providers for the provision of healthcare services. I acknowledge and affirm that:

- I am eighteen (18) years of age or older or am an emancipated minor.
- I signed and executed the accompanying advance directive(s) and did so willingly (or willingly directed another to sign for me) as my free and voluntary act for the purposes therein expressed;
- The information provided is true and accurate to the best of my knowledge.

Signature: ______________________________ Date: ____________________________

Printed Name of Signer: __________________________________

Select the one that applies:

☐ I am the subject of the advance directive.

☐ I have the following relationship to the subject of the advance directive:

State of Arizona

County of ____________________

On this _______ day of __________________, 20____, before me personally appeared ____ (name of signatory), whose identity was proved to me on the basis of satisfactory identification/evidence to be the person whose name is subscribed to this document.

(Seal)

____

Signature of Notary Public

HEALTH CARE POWER OF ATTORNEY
Instructions and Information

GENERAL INSTRUCTIONS: Use this form if you want to select a person, called an "agent", to make future health care decisions for you so that if you become too ill or cannot make those decisions for yourself the person you choose and trust can make medical decisions for you. Be sure you understand the importance of this document. It is a good idea to talk to your doctor and loved ones if you have questions about the type of health care you do or do not want.

AUTOPSY CHOICE: If there is no legal reason to require an autopsy, you can decide if you want one done when you die, or whether you want your agent to choose for you. There is usually a charge for voluntary autopsies. You can help your family and loved ones by making your preferences on this topic clear. For additional information on autopsies please review Arizona Revised Statutes §§ 11-591 and 11-597.

ORGAN DONATION CHOICE (OPTIONAL): You can determine if you want to donate organs or tissues, and if you do, what organs or tissues you want to donate, for what purposes, and to what organizations. You also have the option of whole-body donation for research purposes. You can also choose to have your agent decide. For additional information on Organ Donation, please review Arizona Revised Statutes §§ Title 36, Chapter 7, Article 3 for the laws that pertain to it.

FUNERAL AND BURIAL CHOICE (OPTIONAL): You can determine, your funeral and burial choices in this form. You can select if, upon your death, you would like to be buried and where, or if you would like to be cremated and where your ashes will go, or you can select your agent to make that choice.

If you fill out this form, make sure you **DO NOT SIGN UNTIL** your witness or a notary public is present to watch you sign it.

PLEASE NOTE: At least one adult witness, not to include the proxy if there is one, OR a notary public must witness you signing this document.

DO NOT have the documents signed by both a witness and a notary, just pick one. If you do not know a notary or cannot pay for one, a witness is legally accepted.

Witnesses or notary public CANNOT be anyone who is:
(a) under the age of 18
(b) related to you by blood, adoption, or marriage
(c) entitled to any part of your estate
(d) appointed as your agent
(e) involved in providing your health care at the time this form is signed

OFFICE OF THE ARIZONA ATTORNEY GENERAL
KRIS MAYES

Health Care Power of Attorney

My Information (I am the "Principal"):

Name: ______________________________ Date of Birth: ______________________________

Address: ______________________________ Phone: ______________________________

______________________________ Email: ______________________________

Selection of my health care power of attorney and alternate:

I choose the following person to act as my agent to make health care decisions for me:

Name: ______________________________ Home Phone: ______________________________

Address: ______________________________ Work Phone: ______________________________

______________________________ Cell Phone: ______________________________

I choose the following person to act as an alternate to make health care decisions for me if my first agent is unavailable, unwilling, or unable to make decisions for me:

Name: ______________________________ Home Phone: ______________________________

Address: ______________________________ Work Phone: ______________________________

______________________________ Cell Phone: ______________________________

I AUTHORIZE my agent to make health care decisions for me when I cannot make or communicate my own health care decisions. I want my agent to make all such decisions for me except any decisions that I have expressly stated in this form that I do not authorize him/her to make. My agent should explain to me any choices he or she made if I am able to understand. I further authorize my agent to have access to my "personal protected health care information and medical records". This appointment is effective unless it is revoked by me or by a court order.

Health care decisions that I expressly DO NOT AUTHORIZE if I am unable to make decisions for myself: (Explain or write in "None")

____

____

____

My specific wishes regarding autopsy (additional information on page 1):

*Please note that if not required by law a voluntary autopsy may cost money. Initial your choice.

_____**:** Upon my death I DO NOT consent to a voluntary autopsy.

_____**:** Upon my death I DO consent to a voluntary autopsy.

_____**:** My agent may give or refuse consent for an autopsy.

My specific wishes regarding organ donation (additional information on page 1):

If you do not initial this section your agent may make these decisions for you. Initial your choice.

______: I DO NOT WANT to make an organ or tissue donation, and I DO NOT want this donation authorized on my behalf by my agent or my family.

______: I have already signed a written agreement or donor card regarding donation with the following individual or institution: ______________________________

______: I DO WANT to make an organ or tissue donation when I die. Here are my directions:

1. **What organs/tissues I choose to donate (initial below):**
   a. ______: Whole body
   b. ______: Any needed parts or organs
   c. ______: These parts or organs only:
      i. ______________________________

2. **I am donating organs/tissue for (initial below):**
   a. ______: Any legally authorized purpose
   b. ______: Transplant or therapeutic purposes only
   c. ______: Research only
   d. ______: Other: ______________________________

3. **The organization or person I want my organs/tissue to go to are (initial below):**
   a. ______: ______________________________
   b. ______: Any that my agent chooses

My specific wishes regarding funeral and burial disposition (additional information on page 1):

______: Upon my death, I direct my body to be buried. (Instead of cremated)

______: Upon my death, I direct my body to be buried in: ______________________________

______: Upon my death, I direct my body to be cremated.

______: Upon my death, I direct my body to be cremated with my ashes to be ______________

____

______: My agent will make all funeral and burial decisions.

Do you have a living will?

If you have a Living Will, **you must attach** the Living Will to this form. A blank Living Will is available on the Attorney General's website www.azag.gov. Initial below.

_____: I have SIGNED AND ATTACHED a completed Living Will to this Health Care Power of Attorney.

_____: I have NOT SIGNED a Living Will.

Do you have a POLST (Portable Medical Order)?

A **POLST** form is for when you become seriously ill or frail and toward the end of life. A blank POLST is available on the Attorney General's website www.azag.gov. Initial below.

_____: I have SIGNED AND ATTACHED a completed POLST to this Health Care Power of Attorney.

_____: I have NOT SIGNED a POLST.

Do you have a Prehospital Medical Care Directive – a type of Do Not Resuscitate form (DNR)?

A blank Prehospital Medical Care Directive or DNR is available on the Attorney General's website www.azag.gov. Initial below.

_____: I and my doctor or health care provider HAVE SIGNED a Prehospital Medical Care Directive or DNR on Paper with ORANGE background in the event that Emergency Medical Technicians or hospital emergency personnel are called and my heart or breathing has stopped.

_____: I have NOT SIGNED a Prehospital Medical Care Directive or DNR.

PHYSICIAN AFFIDAVIT (OPTIONAL)

You may wish to ask questions of your physician regarding a particular treatment or about the options in the form. If you do speak with your physician it is a good idea to ask your physician to complete this affidavit and keep a copy for his/her file.

I, Dr. ______________________________ have reviewed this document and have discussed with

________________ any questions regarding the probable medical consequences of the treatment

choices provided above. This discussion with the principal occurred on this day _________________.

I have agreed to comply with the provisions of this directive.

____

Signature of Physician

HIPAA WAIVER OF CONFIDENTIALITY FOR MY AGENT

_____ **(Initial)** I intend for my agent to be treated as I would be with respect to my rights regarding the use and disclosure of my individually identifiable health information or other medical records. This release authority applies to any information governed by the Health Insurance Portability and Accountability Act of 1996 (aka HIPAA), 42 USC 1320d and 45 CFR 160-164.

Revocability of this Health Care Power of Attorney: I retain the right to revoke all or any portion of this form or to disqualify any agent designated by me in this document.

MY SIGNATURE VERIFICATION FOR THE HEALTH CARE POWER OF ATTORNEY

My Signature (Principal): ______________________________ Date: ______________

If you are unable to physically sign this document, your witness/notary may sign and initial for you. If applicable have your witness/notary sign below.

Witness/Notary Verification: The principal of this document directly indicated to me that this Health Care Power of Attorney expresses their wishes and that they intend to adopt it at this time.

Witness/Notary Signature: ____

Name Printed: ______________________________________ Date: ______________

SIGNATURE OF WITNESS (See Page 1 for who CANNOT be a witness)

I was present when this form was signed (or marked). The principal appeared to be of sound mind and was not forced to sign this form. I affirm that I meet the requirements to be a witness as indicated on page one of the health care power of attorney form.

Witness Signature: __________________________________ Date: ______________

Name Printed: ____

Address: ____

OR

SIGNATURE OF NOTARY (See Page 1 for who CANNOT be a Notary)

Notary Public (NOTE: If a witness signs your form, you SHOULD NOT have a notary sign):

NOTORIAL JURAT: Pertains to all five pages of this Health Care Power of Attorney

Dated __________, 20__________.

STATE OF ARIZONA) ss

COUNTY OF ____________)

____

Principal's Name

Subscribed and sworn (or affirmed) before me this __________ day of ________, 20 ______

Notary Public Signature: ______________________________

My Commission Expires: ______________________________

LIVING WILL (End of Life Care)
Instructions

GENERAL INSTRUCTIONS: Use this form to make decisions now about your medical care if you are ever in a terminal condition, a persistent vegetative state or an irreversible coma. You should talk to your doctor about what these terms mean.

The Living Will is your written directions to your health care power of attorney, also referred to as your "agent", your family, your physician, and any other person who might make medical care decisions for you if you are unable to communicate yourself.

It is a good idea to talk to your doctor and loved ones if you have questions about the type of care you do or do not want.

IMPORTANT: If you have a Living Will and a Health Care Power of Attorney, you must attach the Living Will to the Health Care Power of Attorney.

If you fill out this form, make sure you **DO NOT SIGN UNTIL** your witness or a notary public is present to watch you sign it.

PLEASE NOTE: At least one adult witness, not to include the proxy if there is one, OR a notary public must witness you signing this document.

DO NOT have the documents signed by both a witness and a notary, just pick one. If you do not know a notary or cannot pay for one a witness is legally accepted.

Witnesses or notary public CANNOT be anyone who is:
(a) under the age of 18
(b) related to you by blood, adoption, or marriage
(c) entitled to any part of your estate
(d) appointed as your agent
(e) involved in providing your health care at the time this form is signed

OFFICE OF THE ARIZONA ATTORNEY GENERAL
KRIS MAYES

Living Will

My Information (I am the "Principal"):

Name: ______________________________ Date of Birth: ________________________

Address: ____________________________ Phone: _____________________________

____________________________ Email: ______________________________

Some general statements about your health care choices are listed below. If you agree with one of the statements, you should initial that statement. Read all of these statements carefully BEFORE you initial your preferred statement. You can also write your own statement concerning life-sustaining treatment and other matters relating to your health care. You may initial any combination of paragraphs 1, 2, 3 and 4, BUT if you initial paragraph 5 the others should not be initialed.

_____ 1. If I have a terminal condition I do not want my life to be prolonged, and I do not want life-sustaining treatment, beyond comfort care, that would serve only to artificially delay the moment of my death.

***Comfort care is treatment given in an attempt to protect and enhance the quality of life without artificially prolonging life.*

_____ 2. If I am in a terminal condition or an irreversible coma or a persistent vegetative state that my doctors reasonably feel to be irreversible or incurable, I do want the medical treatment necessary to provide care that would keep me comfortable, but I DO NOT want the following:

_____ a. Cardiopulmonary resuscitation (CPR). For example: the use of drugs, electric shock and artificial breathing.

_____ b. Artificially administered food and fluids.

_____ c. To be taken to a hospital if at all avoidable.

_____ 3. Regardless of any other directions I have given in this Living Will, if I am known to be pregnant, I do not want life-sustaining treatment withheld or withdrawn if it is possible that the embryo/fetus will develop to the point of live birth with the continued application of life-sustaining treatment.

_____ 4. Regardless of any other directions I have given in this Living Will, I do want the use of all medical care necessary to treat my condition until my doctors reasonably conclude that my condition is terminal or is irreversible and incurable or I am in a persistent vegetative state.

_____ 5. I want my life to be prolonged to the greatest extent possible (If you initial here, you should not initial any of the others).

PLEASE NOTE: You can attach additional instructions on your medical care wishes that have not been included in this Living Will form. Initial or put a check mark by box A or B below. Be sure to include the attachment if you check B.

_____ A. I HAVE NOT attached additional special instructions about End of Life Care I want.

_____ B. I HAVE attached additional special provisions or limitations about End of Life Care I want.

MY SIGNATURE VERIFICATION FOR THE LIVING WILL

My Signature (Principal): ____________________________________ Date: ________________

If you are unable to physically sign this document your witness/notary may sign and initial for you. If applicable, have your witness/notary sign below.

Witness/Notary Verification: The principal of this document directly indicated to me that this Living Will expresses their wishes and that they intend to adopt it at this time.

Witness/Notary Signature: ____

Name Printed: ____ Date: ________________

SIGNATURE OF WITNESS

I was present when this form was signed (or marked). The principal appeared to be of sound mind and was not forced to sign this form.

Witness Signature: ____ Date: ________________

Name Printed: ____

Address: ____

OR

SIGNATURE OF NOTARY

Notary Public (NOTE: If a witness signs your form, you SHOULD NOT have a notary sign):

NOTORIAL JURAT: Pertains to all three pages of this Living Will

Dated ____________, 20____________.

STATE OF ARIZONA) ss

COUNTY OF ______________)

____

Principals Name

Subscribed and sworn (or affirmed) before me this ___________ day of ________, 20 ______

Notary Public Signature: ____________________________________

My Commission Expires: ____________________

OFFICE OF THE ARIZONA ATTORNEY GENERAL
KRIS MAYES

Mental Health Care Power of Attorney

GENERAL INSTRUCTIONS: Use this form if you want to appoint a person, also referred to as your "agent", to make future mental health care decisions for you if you become incapable of making those decisions for yourself.

The decision about whether you are incapable can only be made by a specialist in neurology or an Arizona licensed psychiatrist or psychologist who will evaluate whether you can give informed consent. Be sure you understand the importance of this document. It is a good idea to talk to your doctor and loved ones if you have questions about the type of mental health care you do or do not want.

If you fill out this form, make sure you **DO NOT SIGN UNTIL** your witness or a notary public is present to watch you sign it. **PLEASE NOTE:** At least one adult witness OR a notary public must witness you signing this document.

DO NOT have the documents signed by both a witness and a notary, just pick one. If you do not know a notary or cannot pay for one, a witness is legally accepted.

Witnesses or notary public CANNOT be anyone who is:
(a) under the age of 18
(b) related to you by blood, adoption, or marriage
(c) entitled to any part of your estate
(d) appointed as your agent
(e) involved in providing your health care at the time this form is signed

My Information (I am the "Principal"):

Name: ______________________________ Date of Birth: ______________________________

Address: ______________________________ Phone: ______________________________

______________________________ Email: ______________________________

Selection of my mental health care power of attorney and alternate:

I choose the following person to act as my agent to make mental health care decisions for me:

Name: ______________________________ Home Phone: ______________________________

Address: ______________________________ Work Phone: ______________________________

______________________________ Cell Phone: ______________________________

I choose the following person to act as an alternate to make mental health care decisions for me if my first agent is unavailable, unwilling, or unable to make decisions for me:

Name: ______________________________ Home Phone: ______________________________

Address: ______________________________ Work Phone: ______________________________

______________________________ Cell Phone: ______________________________

Mental health treatments that I AUTHORIZE if I am unable to make decisions for myself:

Here are the mental health treatments I authorize my agent to make for me if I become incapable of making my own mental health care decisions due to mental or physical illness, injury, disability, or incapacity. This appointment is effective unless and until it is revoked by me or by an order of a court. My agent is authorized to do the following which I have initialed or marked:

_____: To receive medical records and information regarding my mental health treatment and to receive, review, and consent to disclosure of any of my medical records related to that treatment.

_____: To consent to the administration of any medications recommended by my treating physician.

_____: To admit me to an inpatient or partial psychiatric hospitalization program.

_____: Other: ____

____

____

Mental health care treatments that I expressly DO NOT AUTHORIZE if I am unable to make decisions for myself: (Explain or write in "None")

____

____

Revocability of this Mental Health Care Power of Attorney: This mental health care power of attorney or any portion of it may not be revoked and any designated agent may not be disqualified by me during times that I am found to be unable to give informed consent. However, at all other times I retain the right to revoke all or any portion of this mental health care power of attorney or to disqualify any agent designated by me in this document.

HIPAA WAIVER OF CONFIDENTIALITY FOR MY AGENT

_____ **(Initial)** I intend for my agent to be treated as I would be with respect to my rights regarding the use and disclosure of my individually identifiable health information or other medical records. This release of authority applies to any information governed by the Health Insurance Portability and Accountability Act of 1996 (aka HIPAA), 42 USC 1320d and 45 CFR 160-164.

MY SIGNATURE VERIFICATION FOR THE MENTAL HEALTH CARE POWER OF ATTORNEY

My Signature (Principal): ____ Date: __________________

If you are unable to physically sign this document your witness/notary may sign and initial for you. If applicable, have your witness/notary sign below.

Witness/Notary Verification: The principal of this document directly indicated to me that this Health Care Power of Attorney expresses their wishes and that they intend to adopt it at this time.

Witness/Notary Signature: ____

Name Printed: ____ Date: __________________

SIGNATURE OF WITNESS (See Page 1 for who CANNOT be a witness)

I was present when this form was signed (or marked). The principal appeared to be of sound mind and was not forced to sign this form. I affirm that I meet the requirements to be a witness as indicated on page one of the mental health care power of attorney form.

Witness Signature: ____ Date: _________________

Name Printed: ____

Address: ____

OR

SIGNATURE OF NOTARY (See Page 47 for who CANNOT be a Notary)

Notary Public (NOTE: If a witness signs your form, you SHOULD NOT have a notary sign):

<u>NOTORIAL JURAT:</u> Pertains to all three pages of this State of Arizona Mental Health Care Power of Attorney dated _____________, 20_____________.

STATE OF ARIZONA) ss

COUNTY OF _______________)

____

Principal's Name

Subscribed and sworn (or affirmed) before me this ____________ day of _________, 20 _______

Notary Public Signature: ____

My Commission Expires: ____

Last Wishes101
DISCOVER PEACE OF MIND

Last Will and Testament

(Page)

For: ____________________
(name of person)

LAST WILL AND TESTAMENT OF ____________________ **Dated**______________

I, ________________________ whose address is __________________________________
__________________________, declare that this is my Last Will and Testament and I revoke all previous wills.

My marital status is that ______________________________.

I have ____________ child(ren) living. My child(ren)'s name addresses and birthdates are as follows:

____
____
____
____
____

I have ____________ grandchild(ren) living. My grandchild(ren)'s names, addresses, and birthdates are as follows:

____
____
____
____
____
____

I make the following specific gifts:

____
____
____
____
____
____
____
____

Testator's Initials: ___________________

Last Wishes101

DISCOVER PEACE OF MIND

Last Will and Testament

For: ______________________

(name of person)

(Page)

I give all the rest of my property, whether real or personal, wherever located, to:
____, my
________________________or if not surviving, to ____________,
my_______________________________.

All beneficiaries named in this will must survive me by thirty (30) days to receive any gifts under this Will. If any beneficiary and I should die simultaneously, I shall be conclusively presumed to have survived that beneficiary for the purpose of this will. I appoint______________ , my ________________________ of _____________________________ as Executor, to serve without bond. If not surviving or unable to survive, I appoint ____________________, my ____________________ of ________________________________ as Alternate Executor, also to serve without bond. In addition to any powers, authority, and discretion granted by law, I grant such Executor or Alternate Executor any and all powers to perform any acts, in his/her sole discretion and without court approval for the management and distribution of my estate, including independent administration of my estate.

If a Guardian is needed for my/any of my minor child(ren). I appoint:

________________________________,

My ___________________ of ___________________________ as Guardian of the person(s) and property of my/any of my minor child(ren) to serve without bond.

If not surviving or unable to serve, I appoint ________________________________, my _____________________ of _______________________________ as Alternate Guardian, also to serve without bond. In addition to any powers, authority, and discretion granted by the Guardian or Alternate Guardian any and all powers to perform any acts, in his/her sole discretion and without court approval, for the management and distribution of the property of my/any of my child(ren). If my/any of my child(ren) is/are under _____ years of age, upon my death. I direct that any property that I give him/her/them under this Will be held in an individual trust for my/each child(ren) under the following terms until he/she each shall reach _______ years of age.

In addition to all powers, authority, and discretion granted by law, I grant such Trustee or Alternate Trustee full power to perform any acts, in his/her sole discretion and without court approval, to distribute and manage the assets of any such trust. In the Trustee's sole discretion, the Trustee may distribute any or all of the principal, income, or both, any of such trust as deemed necessary for the beneficiary's health, support, welfare, and education. Any income not distributed shall be added to the trust principal.

Testators Initials: ____________________

Last Wishes101
DISCOVER PEACE OF MIND

Last Will and Testament

For: ____________________
(name of person)

(Page)

In addition to all powers, authority, and discretion granted by law, I hereby grant the Trustee or Alternate Trustee full authority to perform any necessary acts without requiring court approval for the distribution and management of the assets within any such trust. The Trustee may, at their sole discretion, distribute any or all of the principal, income, or both, from the trust as deemed necessary for the beneficiary's health, support, welfare, and education. Any undistributed income shall be added to the trust principal.

The trust shall terminate upon the beneficiary reaching the specified age, upon the beneficiary's death prior to reaching the specified age, or upon the distribution of all trust funds. Upon termination, any remaining undistributed principal and income shall pass to the beneficiary. If the beneficiary does not survive, the remaining assets shall pass to the beneficiary's heirs, or if none survive, to the residue of my estate.

I publish and sign this last Will and Testament, consisting of ____________ pages, on ____________________, 20___, and declare that I do freely, for the purposes expressed, under no constraint or undue influence and that I am of sound mind and legal age,

______________________	______________	______________
Signature of Testator	Date	Printed name of Testator

We, the undersigned, being the first sworn on oath and under penalty of perjury state that: On ____________________________________, 20 _________, in the presence of all of us, ________________________ the Testator published and signed this Last Will and Testament, and then at Testator's request, and in Testator's presence, we all signed below as witnesses, and we declare, under penalty of perjury, that, to the best of our knowledge, the Testator signed

This instrument is freely, under no constraint or undue influence, and is of sound mind and legal age.

Testator's Initials: ______________

Last Wishes101
DISCOVER PEACE OF MIND

Last Will and Testament

For: ____________________
(name of person)

(Page)

We, the undersigned, being the first sworn on oath and under penalty of perjury state that: On ________________________________, 20 _________, in the presence of all of us, _______________________ the Testator published and signed this Last Will and Testament, and then at Testator's request, and in Testator's presence, we all signed below as witnesses, and we declare, under penalty of perjury, that, to the best of our knowledge, the Testator signed

This instrument is freely, under no constraint or undue influence, and is of sound mind and legal age.

_____________________________________ _________________________________

Signature of Witness #1 Printed name of Witness #1

_____________________________________ _________________________________

Signature of Witness #2 Printed name of Witness #2

_____________________________________ _________________________________

Signature of Witness #3 Printed name of Witness #3

Notary Acknowledgement

State _____________________________ County of ________________________________

On _______________, 20 _______, the Testator,

____________________________________ And _________________________________,

_________________, __________________ The witnesses personally came before me and being duly sworn, did state that they are the persons described in the above document and they signed the above document in my presence as a free and voluntary act for the purposes stated.

____

Signature of Notary Public

Notary Public, in and for the county of _______________ Notary Seal Sate of ________________. My commission expires _______________.

Testator's Initials: __________________

Last Wishes101
DISCOVER PEACE OF MIND

Last Will and Testament

For: ______________________
(name of person)

(Page)

LAST WILL AND TESTAMENT OF ______________________ Date __________

I, ____________________ whose address is ______________________

____________________________, declare that this is my Last Will Testament and I revoke all previous wills.

My marital status is that ___________________________.

I have ______________________ child(ren) living. My child(ren)'s name addresses and birthdates are as follows:

I have __________ grandchild(ren) living, My grandchild(ren)'s names, addresses and birthdates are as follows:

I make the following specific gifts:

Testator's Initials: __________________

Last Will and Testament For: ________________

(name of person)

(Page)

I give all the rest of my property, whether real or personal, wherever located, to: ____, my _______________ or if not surviving, to ________________________ my ________________________________.

All beneficiaries named in this Will must survive me by thirty (30) days to receive any gift under this Will. If any beneficiary and I should die simultaneously, I shall be conclusively presumed to have survived that beneficiary for purposes of this Will. I appoint: ____________________, my ____________________of __________________________________ as Executor, to serve without bond. If not surviving or unable to serve, I appoint: ________________________, my ________________________ of ____ as Alternate Executor, also to serve without bond. In addition to any powers, authority, and discretion granted by law, I grant such Executor or Alternate Executor full authority to perform any necessary acts, at their sole discretion and without requiring court approval, for the management and distribution of my estate, including independent administration of my estate.

If a Guardian is needed for my/any of my minor child(ren). I appoint: ________________________________, my ______________________of ____ as Guardian of the person(s) and property of my/any of my minor child(ren) to serve without bond.

If not surviving or unable to survive, I appoint:____________________, my ___________________________ of _________________________as Alternative Executor, also to serve without bond. In addition to any powers, authority, and discretion granted by law, I grant such Executor or Alternative Executor any and all powers to perform any acts, in his/her sole discretion and without court approval, for the management and distribution of the property of my/any of my child(ren). If my/any of my child(ren) is/are ______ years of age, upon my death, I direct that any property that I give him/her/them under this Will be held in an individual trust for my/each child(ren) under the following terms until he/she each shall reach ___________ years of age.

Testator's Initials_____________

Last Wishes101
DISCOVER PEACE OF MIND

Last Will and Testament For: ____________________

(name of person)

(Page)

In addition, I appoint ______________________________, my ____________________ of ________________________ as trustee of any and all required trusts, to serve without bond. If not surviving, or otherwise unable to serve, then I appoint ______________________, my __________________________ of ______________________________ as Alternate Trustee, also serve without bond.

In addition, I appoint _______________________, my __________________ of __________________________ as trustee of any and all required trusts, to serve without bond. If not surviving, or otherwise unable to serve, then I appoint _______________________ my ___________________________ of ________________________________ as Alternate Trustee, also to serve without bond.

In addition to all powers, authority, and discretion granted by law, I authorize the Trustee or Alternate Trustee to exercise full discretion, without requiring court approval, in managing and distributing the assets of any such trust.

The Trustee may, in their sole discretion, distribute any or all of the principal, income, or both, from the trust as deemed necessary for the beneficiary's health, support, welfare, and education. Any income not distributed shall accrue to the trust principal.

The trust shall terminate upon the beneficiary reaching the required age, upon the beneficiary's death prior to reaching the required age, or upon the complete distribution of all trust funds. Upon termination, any remaining undistributed principal and income shall pass to the beneficiary. If the beneficiary does not survive, these assets shall pass to the beneficiary's heirs, or if none exist, to the residue of my estate.

Testator's Initials______________

Last Wishes101
DISCOVER PEACE OF MIND

Last Will and Testament

For: ______________________
(name of person)

(Page)

I publish and sign this Last Will and Testament, consisting of ________ pages, on ________________ 20 ______, and declare that I do freely, for the purposes expressed under no constraint or undue influence, and that I am of sound mind and legal age,

______________________________ ________________________

Signature of Testator   Date   Printed name of Testators

We, the undersigned, being first sworn on oath and under penalty of perjury state that:

On __________________________, 20______, in the presence of all of us,______________________ the Testators published and signed this Last Will and Testament, and then at Testators request, and in the Testator's presence, and in each other's presence.

We all sign below as witnesses, and we declare, under penalty of perjury, that to the best of our knowledge, the Testator signed this instrument freely, under no constraint or undue influence, and is of sound mind and legal age.

______________________________ ________________________

Signature of Witness # 1   Printed name of Witness # 1

______________________________ ________________________

Signature of Witness # 2   Printed name of Witness # 2

______________________________ ________________________

Signature of Witness # 3   Printed name of Witness # 3

Notary Acknowledgement

State ___________________________ County of _________________

On ___________, 20 _______, the Testator, ___________________ And _____________________, _____________________, ____________________ the witnesses, personally came before me and being duly sworn, did state that they are the persons described in the above documents and they signed the above document in my presence as a free and voluntary act for the purposes stated.

____

Signature of Notary Public

Notary Public, in and for the County of _______________ Notary Seal

State of __________________. My commission expires_____________.

Testator's Initials_____________

Last Wishes101
DISCOVER PEACE OF MIND

Distribution of Treasured Possessions

For: ____________
(name of person)

Print only on the front side of this of this page.

ITEM: ______________________ Description: ______________________
Special instructions for disposition: ______________________
____

ITEM: ______________________ Description: ______________________
Special instructions for disposition: ______________________
____

ITEM: ______________________ Description: ______________________
Special instructions for disposition: ______________________
____

ITEM: ______________________ Description: ______________________
Special instructions for disposition: ______________________
____

ITEM: ______________________ Description: ______________________
Special instructions for disposition: ______________________
____

ITEM: ______________________ Description: ______________________
Special instructions for disposition: ______________________
____

ITEM: ______________________ Description: ______________________
Special instructions for disposition: ______________________
____

Last Wishes101
DISCOVER PEACE OF MIND

Important Documents

For: ____________________
(name of person)

Copies attached or location: ____

Graduation certificates: ____

Military Discharge: ____

Wedding License: ____

Deeds: ____

Patents: ____

Auto Titles: ____

Stock Certificates, Bonds, Annuities ______________________________________

Will, Living Will ____

Others:

Last Wishes101
DISCOVER PEACE OF MIND

Insurance Policies:

For: ____________________
(name of person)

Life Insurance Policy
Company: ______________________________ Agent: ______________________
Phone: ____________________ Policy#: ______________________________
Premium: ____

Home Owners Insurance Covering Home
At Address: ____
Company: ___________________________ Agent: ______________________
Phone: ______________________ Policy#: ____________________________
Premium: ____

Auto Insurance Covering Vehicles
Listed Vehicles: ____
Company: ___________________________ Agent: ______________________
Phone: ______________________ Policy#: ____________________________
Premium: ____

Hospitalization Policy
Company: __________________________________ Agent: _________________
Phone: __________________________ Policy#: _________________________
Premium: ____
Other Insurance: Dental, Nursing Home, Pet, Burial, etc.

Last Wishes101
DISCOVER PEACE OF MIND

Facebook Memorial:

For: ____________________
(name of person)

When a Facebook member passes on, his information remains taken off or changed. This form will memorize the deceased.

Upon my death, please permanently delete my current Facebook account and convert it into a Memorialization Account in my name.

Signature ________________________ **Date:** ___________

Memorialization Request:

Full name as it appears on the account: __________________________________ Email Address listed on the account: _____________________________________ Web address of my timeline: ____
Relationship of the person who is authorized to delete my Facebook Account _____________ Immediate family (spouse, parent, sibling, child)
_____________ Extended family (grandparent, aunt, uncle, cousin)
_____________ Non-family (friend, co-worker, classmate)
_____________ Other (relationship): ________________________

Note: Facebook will require proof of death. Generally, they request a line to an obituary. Please have this ready when completing the online Memorization form on Facebook.com

Email contact for Authorization party: __________________________

Name of the Authorization party: ______________________________

Last Wishes101

DISCOVER PEACE OF MIND

BURIAL INSURANCE:

Burial insurance is a specialized insurance product designed to cover the costs associated with funerals and burials. It offers financial protection to the family of the policyholder after their passing, easing the financial strain typically associated with funeral arrangements. This enables loved ones to focus on mourning and honoring the memory of the deceased, rather than worrying about managing the expenses.

A key benefit of burial insurance is its ability to allow individuals to plan ahead and ensure that their final expenses are taken care of. By obtaining a burial insurance policy, individuals can have peace of mind knowing that their family members will not be burdened with the financial obligations related to funeral and burial costs. This is especially valuable for older individuals who may not have sufficient savings set aside for these expenses.

Another benefit of burial insurance is its accessibility. Unlike conventional life insurance policies, burial insurance generally does not necessitate a medical exam or extensive health screening. This makes it a feasible choice for individuals with health conditons that might prevent them from qualifying for tradi onal life insurance coverage.

Burial insurance policies often feature lower premiums compared to traditional life insurance policies, which makes them a more affordable op on. Moreover, many burial insurance plans provide flexible payment terms, allowing policyholders to choose a payment schedule that aligns with their financial circumstances.

Laugh Matters

A couple in their nineties were both having problems remembering things. During a checkup, the doctor told them that they we're physically okay, but might want to start writing things down to help them remember. Later that night, while watching TV, the old man got up from his chair. 'Want anything while I'm in the kitchen?' he asked. "Will you get me a bowl of ice cream?" "Sure." "Don't you think you should write it down so you can remember it?" she asked. "No, I can remember it." "Well, I'd like some strawberries on top, too. Maybe you should write it down, so as not to forget it" "He said, "I can remember that. You want a bowl of ice cream with strawberries." "I'd also like whipped cream. I'm certain you'll forget that - write it down?" she asked. Irritated, he said, "I don't need to write it down, I can remember it! Ice cream with strawberries and whipped cream - I got it, for goodness's sake!" Then he toddled off into the kitchen. After about 20 minutes, the old man returned and handed his wife a plate of bacon and eggs. She stared at the plate for a moment.

"Where's my toast?"

Last Wishes101
DISCOVER PEACE OF MIND

Five Compelling Reasons to Consider a Final Expense Life Insurance Policy:

Final expense insurance offers comprehensive life insurance coverage tailored to your needs. Here are five compelling reasons to consider a final expense insurance policy:

1. **Lifetime Protection**: Final expense life insurance ensures lifelong coverage with a guaranteed death benefit. It also builds cash value over time, providing added financial security.

2. **Coverage for Funeral and Final Expenses**: Proper planning and adequate life insurance coverage can help your family cover funeral and burial costs. Additionally, having sufficient coverage can assist in settling any remaining final expenses, freeing you from all worries.

3. **Easy Qualification Options**: Final expense insurance offers level, graded, and guaranteed issue coverage, making it accessible to nearly everyone seeking life insurance. High-risk health conditions that might lead to rejection with traditional underwriting can often be accommodated with guaranteed issue policies.

4. **No Medical Exam Required**: One of the key advantages of final expense insurance is the absence of a medical exam during the application process. This eliminates the need for appointments with medical examiners, needles, urinalysis, or blood pressure readings.

5. **Fast Approval Process**: Because final expense insurance skips the medical exam, approval typically relies on answering medical questions to determine eligibility. This streamlined process ensures quicker approval times, allowing you to secure life insurance promptly.

In summary, final expense insurance provides valuable financial support by covering funeral and burial expenses, thereby easing the financial burden on loved ones during a challenging time. It's essential for individuals to assess their options carefully and select a final expense insurance policy that aligns with their specific needs and financial circumstances.

Funeral Cost Summary:

Funeral Home's General Price List (GPL)

The Federal Trade Commission oversees funeral homes and enforces regulations known as The Funeral Rule. This rule ensures that consumers have the right to purchase funeral goods and services individually. You are not obligated to accept a package that includes items you do not wish to purchase. Every funeral home is required to maintain a General Price List (GPL), which is a detailed, itemized list of all available goods and services. The GPL serves as a tool for comparing funeral costs within your local area.

A few funeral homes publish their GPL online. As consumers become more informed and insist on more price transparency, more funeral homes will publish their GPL online. If you don't see the GPL as part of the funeral home's website call or email them and ask them to send you a copy.

This is a rough guide for how much funeral services and products typically cost as provided by the National Funeral Directors Association's statistics.

Funeral Home's Basic Services Fee

The basic services fee encompasses essential services that are standard across all funeral homes. This fee covers activities such as the initial meeting to plan the funeral, preparation, and submission of necessary authorizations and permits, and coordination of arrangements with cemeteries, crematories, or other third parties. It also includes overhead costs such as professional licensing, legal and accounting fees, insurance, building maintenance, utilities, parking lot upkeep, grounds maintenance, and administrative expenses. Customers must pay the basic services fee in addition to any specific services they request. Unless a package or service explicitly includes the basic services fee in its stated price, assume that the fee will be added to the total bill.

As with all funeral home services, there is a huge range in how much funeral homes charge for their basic services fee.

- Low-priced basic service fees range from $480 to $695
- Medium-priced basic service fees range from $1,205 to $1,880
- High-priced basic service fees range from $2,200 to $3,000

Quick Tip

Final expense insurance is a basic life insurance policy that covers people till they reach the age of 100. It is an easy insurance to obtain, much simpler than complicated whole-life or term policies. Burial insurance or final expense insurance policy allows your loved ones to cover the expenses of a funeral with the flexibility to choose how to use the existing policy at the time of a loved one's death. Besides the peace of mind that a final expense insurance policy offers, it also offers never-changing premiums, a policy that accumulates a cash value and permanent coverage making it a wise investment decision for your future.

The National Funeral Director's Association's 2006 survey found that the average funeral home basic service fee was $ 1,595.

Last Wishes101
DISCOVER PEACE OF MIND

Funeral Package Fees:

Traditional Burial Package Fees

The traditional burial package typically covers the retrieval of the deceased from the place of death, embalming, preparation for visitation (including dressing, cosmetology, and placing in the casket), temporary storage, visitation or viewing, a formal funeral ceremony, and transportation of the body to the cemetery.

The contents of a traditional burial package can vary significantly, primarily depending on whether the package price includes a casket and vault. The price ranges provided below do not incorporate the cost of a casket or vault.

- Low-priced traditional packages range from $2,620 to $3,000
- Medium-priced traditional packages range from $3,200 to $4,700
- High-priced traditional package range from $5,000 to $6,000

Alert!

The funeral home package will not include the cemetery fees for the plot, grave opening and closing, or the grave marker.

Direct Burial Package Fees

A direct burial package entails a burial without a formal service or ceremony, often without embalming the body. When considering a direct burial package, ensure it covers the basic services fee, storage fee, the cost of the casket, and transportation to the cemetery.

Please note, that the funeral home's package does not encompass cemetery fees such as plot expenses, grave opening and closing fees, or the grave marker.

- Low-priced direct packages range from $1,000 to $1,400
- Medium-priced direct packages range from $1,600 to $1,800
- High-priced direct packages range from $2,000 to $3,600

Quick Tip!

Wal-Mart has started selling coffins on its Web site at prices that undercut funeral homes. The move follows a similar one by discount rival Costco, which also sells coffins on its site

Direct cremation

It typically involves minimal costs for the cremation procedure itself, which generally ranges between $175 to $300 at crematories. However, additional services and products are typically required in conjunction with the cremation process. These may include engaging a funeral home to collect the body from the place of death and transport it to the crematory, arranging for the crematory or funeral home to place the ashes into an urn, storing the urn until it is picked up, and securing the requisite legal authorizations and permits for the cremation process.

You'll also need a cremation container for the body (often a fiberboard or cardboard casket) and something to place the ashes in (usually an urn).

When opting for cremation, you will also require a container for the body, often a fiberboard or cardboard casket, and an urn for the ashes.

Most funeral homes offer a direct cremation package that includes essential products and services for cremation. Surprisingly, some funeral homes may provide a package that covers everything except the actual cremation cost. This is because the funeral home does not operate the crematory; instead, the crematory fee is added to the funeral home's cremation package.

When evaluating a cremation package, ensure it covers the basic services fee, fees for body removal, the cremation container, the cremation procedure itself, a container for the cremated remains, and storage of the remains until they are picked up.
You'll notice direct cremation packages have a huge variation in price.

- Low-priced direct cremation packages range from $500 to $800 and are offered by crematories or funeral homes with their own crematory.
- Medium-priced direct cremation packages range from $1,000 to $1,500.
- High-priced direct cremation packages range from $1,800 to $3,000.

! Alert!

Shockingly, many funeral homes will offer a cremation package that provides everything but the cost of the actual cremation! This is because the funeral home doesn't own the crematory. The crematory's fee for the cremation is added to the cost of the funeral homes' cremation package.

Urns

Cremated remains (ashes) are not a biohazard and don't require any special container. Most people choose to purchase a special container for the ashes called an urn. There are countless urns available to purchase online. Basic wood and metal urns start at around $100.

Engraving is an option to personalize the urn with a name, a date, or a phrase of your choice, but this will be an additional charge.

- Low-priced urns range from $80 to $200
- Medium-priced urns range from $250 to $350
- High-priced urns range from $400 to $2,000

Did You Know?

According to the 2012 annual report from the Cremation Association of North America, cost was a primary factor influencing people to choose cremation over burial. While there are instances where cremation costs can exceed those of burial, typically cremation is less expensive. On average nationally, burial costs around $7,300, inclusive of embalming, casket, vault, and other commonly requested services, whereas cremation averages $1,650.

Last Wishes101
DISCOVER PEACE OF MIND

Wood & Metal Casket Costs

Wood caskets span from straightforward pine boxes to intricately crafted old-growth mahogany. Similarly, metal caskets range from 18-gauge steel to options in copper and bronze.

- Low-priced plain wood caskets range from $345 to $800
- Medium-priced finished wood and metal caskets range from $1,000 to $3,000
- High-priced finished wood and metal caskets range from $3,500 to $12,000

The National Funeral Director's Association's 2006 survey found that the average funeral home price for a metal casket was $2,255.

- High-priced finished wood and metal caskets range from $3,500 to $12,000

Burial Vault Costs:

Burial vaults, also known as grave liners, are typically required by most cemeteries for interring caskets. These sturdy, rectangular containers are commonly made of materials such as concrete, metal (steel or bronze), or composite plastic, designed to be durable and long-lasting with warranties often extending over 100 years.

The primary purpose of burial vaults is to preserve the cemetery's landscape. Without a vault, a casket can deteriorate and collapse over time, causing depressions in the ground and potentially tilting headstones. Vaults ensure the cemetery grounds remain even and aesthetically pleasing, while also facilitating safe and efficient maintenance with heavy equipment like lawnmowers and backhoes.

- Low-priced vaults range from $795 to $1,000.
- Medium-priced vaults range from $1,000 to $2,000.
- High-priced caskets range from $2,000 to $14,000 according to The National Funeral Directors Association

Quick Tip

When acquiring a cemetery plot, be sure to inquire about:

- Are additional lots required for purchase?
- Where is the location and cost of the plot?
- Is perpetual care an additional cost?
- What are the fees for opening and closing each grave?
- Are specific memorials required to be purchased from the cemetery?
- How much does it cost to set up memorials?
- Is a vault mandatory, even for cremated remains? Can it be bought elsewhere?
- Are there restrictions on markers or planting?
- What are the administrative fees?
- Who is the owner of the cemetery?
- Are there municipal or religious cemeteries nearby that offer comparable services at lower costs?

Purchase a Casket

Wal-Mart, the world's largest retailer, now offers coffins for sale on its website, aiming to retain customers even after their passing. This move mirrors a similar strategy by discount competitor Costco, which also sells caskets online.

Based in Bentonville, Ark., Wal-Mart has introduced approximately 15 casket
options and numerous urns on its website. Prices range from $999 for steel models like "Dad Remembered" and "Mom Remembered" to the mid-range $1,699
"Executive Privilege." Most caskets are priced below $2,000, with the exception of the Sienna Bronze Casket at $3,199. Orders ship within 48 hours, and federal law mandates that funeral homes must accept third-party caskets.

These coffins are sourced from Star Legacy Funeral Network, Inc., headquartered in McHenry, Ill., which sells similar caskets at comparable or lower prices on its own website, alongside a wide selection of other funeral products.

Legacy CEO Rick Obadiah mentioned that the response to the venture has exceeded expectations for both his company and Walmart, although he declined to provide specific details. A spokesperson from Walmart.com also chose not to disclose sales figures and played down the initiative.

Obadiah stated that walmart.com will eventually offer over 200 Star Legacy products, including pet urns and memorial jewelry, with plans to introduce approximately two dozen caskets. Additionally, Star Legacy supplies similar products to online retailer Overstock.com and urns to Costco's website.

Part of their business strategy involves encouraging advance planning:
Walmart.com allows customers to finance casket purchases over 12 months with no interest.

! Alert!

Obituary Fraud & Scams:

Thieves and fraudsters can gather information from obituaries. Avoid disclosing the address of the deceased. Ensure someone stays at home during the funeral to prevent potential burglaries.

Exercise caution with individuals who claim the deceased owed them money. Request proof of delivery of goods or services before the death occurred.

Check the deceased's calendar for upcoming purchases or appointments and cancel them to prevent unauthorized charges. A death certificate may be required for cancellation purposes.

Last Wishes101
DISCOVER PEACE OF MIND

MAUSOLEUM, HEADSTONE COST, GRAVE COST

Factors That Affect the Cost of a Headstone, Cemetery Memorial, Monument or Mausoleum

By ROME MONUMENT

Flat Granite Grave Markers

Flat, flush, or lawn-level grave markers are precision cut slabs of granite that lie flat on the ground at the head or foot of a grave. We often use classic or traditional design elements to enhance the beauty and personalize the message on the marker. They can be for any number of traditional and cremation graves and come in a variety of sizes, styles, shapes, and granite colors.

Single Classic Flat Granite Markers: $300 to $2700

Double Classic Flat Granite Markers: $600 to $4200

Bevel/Pillow Granite Grave Markers

Bevel, or pillow, markers are cut slabs of granite that are raised slightly above the ground and are higher in the back than in the front. This makes them easier to locate and read from a distance in a cemetery. Sometimes they have a granite base to support the marker. We use classic or traditional design elements to enhance the beauty and personalize the message on the marker. They can be for any number of traditional and cremation graves and come in a variety of sizes, styles, shapes, and colors.

Single Classic Bevel/Pillow Granite Markers: $600 to $3500

Double Classic Bevel/Pillow Granite Markers: $800 to $6000

Flat Bronze Grave Markers

Last Wishes101
DISCOVER PEACE OF MIND

Flat Bronze Grave Markers lie flat on the ground at the head or foot of grave. The bronze is actually a flat plate that can be affixed to the face of an optional flat granite marker. They often feature raised artistic design elements to enhance the beauty and personalize the message on the headstone. Flat bronze grave markers can be for any number of traditional and cremation graves and come in a variety of sizes, styles, shapes, and colors.

Single Bronze Markers: $995 to $4100
Double Bronze Markers: $2800 to $6500

Bronze Veterans Markers & Bronze Matching Markers for Spouses

The government provides bronze grave markers to veterans but not to their spouses - unless they're both buried in a qualified government cemetery. Fortunately, veterans' family members can order an exact matching bronze marker design with your personal information to go side by side in a private cemetery. We design perfect copies that can complement or take the place of a marker issued by the Department of Veterans Affairs. We also make markers for the veterans themselves.

Matching Bronze Veterans Markers for Spouses: Starting from $995

Double Crypt Mausoleums

A double crypt mausoleum contains two crypts to store two caskets, generally a husband and wife, spouses, or significant others. These companion crypts can be placed back to back, side by side, or one

on top of the other. The front is typically decorated with lettering, symbols and artwork. You can select from a wide variety of styles, shapes, and granite colors in different price ranges.

Basic Family Small Double-Crypt Private Mausoleums: From $23K

Two Crypt 'Stacked' (One On Top Of The Other) Mausoleums: From $23K

Companion Crypt Mausoleums: From $23K

Side-By-Side Couch Crypt Mausoleums: From $23K

Private Family Multiple Crypt Mausoleums

-Crypt Mausoleum

Private family multiple crypt mausoleums contain crypts for not only a husband and wife, but for other family members as well. Families often have Rome build a structure that initially encases one or two crypts but that has room for many more crypts for many more family members. The front is typically decorated with lettering, symbols and artwork. You can select from a wide variety of granite colors in different price ranges. 3 Crypt Mausoleums: Starting From $28K

4 Crypt Mausoleums: Starting From $40K
6 Crypt Mausoleums: Starting From $55K

Private Family Multiple Crypt Mausoleums

2-Crypt Walk-In Mausoleum

Walk-in mausoleums are buildings that contain the crypt or crypts of many family members. They have doors and interior space for visitors to be comfortable and protected from the elements year round. Inside your mausoleum, you can display photographs, murals, and personal artifacts that tell the story of your life.

Walk-In Mausoleum (2-4 Crypts): Starting From $85K
(6-8 Crypts): Starting From $145K
Estate Walk-In Mausoleum (12-16 Crypts): Starting From $350K

Last Wishes101
DISCOVER PEACE OF MIND

Commemorative Memorial Plaques

Custom commemorative plaques can also be affixed to traditional or cremation monuments such as benches, boulders, flat or upright monuments, columbarium niche doors, and statues. They can also mark the site where cremated remains are buried or be attached to a wall or tree as an everlasting reminder of an individual's life. Made of granite, bronze and other metals, you can select from a wide variety of metallic and granite colors in a variety of shapes, styles, and in different price ranges.

Commemorative Memorial Plaques: Priced per Desired Size

Other Headstone, Monument & Memorial Prices

- Vestibule Mausoleums (Small Structures, Resembling A House or Small Ornate Building With a Door In the Middle): Starting From $87K
- Cemetery Owned Outdoor Mausoleums (32 Crypt Community Mausoleum, Not A Walk-In): Starting from $150K
- Cemetery Owned Walk-In Mausoleums (32 Crypt Community Building): Starting from$275K
- Westminster Family Crypts (4-Crypt Mausoleum, Side-By Side Crypts, and Stacked On Top of Each Other): Starting from $35K

Rome Monument also sells community mausoleums, private columbarium's, church and community columbarium's, crypts, urns and niche nameplates and plaques.

Memorial and Headstone Options

Listed below are a number of general memorial and headstone options to enhance your memorial. For most lettering and artwork on the face of the headstone, there is no extra charge.

- Personalized Engravings
- Classic Carvings and Images
- Etched Portraits
- Etched Scenes and Images
- Epitaph Inscriptions

- Diamond Etched Portraits – Extra Charge
- Diamond Etched Scenes and Images – Extra Charge
- Flower and Floral Vases – Extra Charge
- Bronze Lettering, Accents and Attachments – Extra Charge

FOR INFORMATION ABOUT THESE PRODUCTS Contact: Rome Monument 300 West Park Street
Rochester, PA 15074
Phone (724) 770-0100
Fax: (724) 770-9835
Email: info@romemonuments.com

Last Wishes101
DISCOVER PEACE OF MIND

Veterans Funeral & Burial Benefits

All veterans are eligible for burial in a national cemetery, a grave marker (applicable at any cemetery), and a flag. Spouses and dependent children are entitled to a lot and marker, but only in a national cemetery. There are no fees for opening or closing the grave, providing a vault or liner, or setting the marker in a national cemetery. However, depending on the circumstances, families may be responsible for all other expenses, including transportation to the cemetery.

• In the event of death during active duty, all funeral expenses including body preparation, casket, transportation to the place of disposition, interment (if in a national cemetery), and marker will be covered by the military. Additionally, effective July 2005, next-of-kin are entitled to a death gratuity of $100,000, retroactive to October 7, 2001.

• In cases of death resulting from a service-related injury, eligible veterans receive a $2,000 burial allowance. This allowance can be used to cover certain funeral director expenses, the cost of a casket, and transportation to the cemetery. If the death occurred in a VA facility, transportation of the body to the cemetery will be paid for, provided the distance does not exceed that of the veteran's last place of residence.

If burial does not take place in a national cemetery, there is a $300 interment allowance available. However, it is unlikely to cover the costs associated with opening and closing the grave or vault charges, let alone the expense of purchasing the burial plot. While a marker is provided at no charge, private cemeteries typically impose a setting fee for placement.

• In cases of non-service-related death occurring in a VA facility or while collecting VA pension or disability compensation, eligible veterans are entitled to a $300 burial allowance. This allowance may be utilized to offset certain standard funeral expenses.

For veterans eligible for burial in a national cemetery, the burial itself is provided at no cost. However, all additional mortuary expenses are the responsibility of the family. Transportation to a

Did You Know?

A spouse and dependents of an eligible veteran are entitled to burial in a national cemetery even if the veteran is not buried there. A spouse who remarries a nonveteran may claim burial rights from the prior marriage.

Military honors or a funeral honor guard may be available from nearby military installations or veterans groups. A flag is provided on request for the burial of any veteran.

Apply through the VA and pick up at a U.S. Post Office

national cemetery, not exceeding the distance to the deceased's residence, is arranged only if death occurs in a VA facility.

When burial takes place in a location other than a national cemetery, a $300 interment allowance is available. It should be noted that this allowance is typically insufficient to cover expenses such as the opening and closing of the grave, vault charges, and the cost of the burial plot. Additionally, while a marker is provided free of charge, private cemeteries may impose a fee for its installation.

In the event of a veteran's death outside a VA facility and not receiving military pension or compensation, certain burial benefits are available. These include eligibility for a burial plot in a national cemetery, any necessary vault, interment, a marker, and a flag.

However, if interment occurs in a cemetery other than a national cemetery, the family assumes responsibility for purchasing the burial plot, covering costs for opening and closing the grave, acquiring a vault if required, and paying any fees associated with setting the government-issued marker if selected. All other funeral expenses must also be covered by the family.

Spouse and Dependents

- Spouses and dependents of eligible veterans have the right to burial in a national cemetery, regardless of whether the veteran is interred there.
- A spouse who remarries a nonveteran retains burial eligibility from their prior marriage. Spouses receiving military pay and passing away in a military medical facility qualify for military transportation to the nearest national cemetery or to their last permanent residence.
- Adult children of veterans are eligible for burial benefits only if they are disabled and dependent.

Other Eligible Individuals

A variety of individuals qualify for veterans' burial benefits based on their military-related service. This includes civilians who contributed to military efforts during wartime, members of the National Guard and Reserves with a minimum of 20 years of service, and certain

Did You Know?

For veterans who passed away on or after September 11, 2001, the government offers a headstone even if a private marker is already present on the grave.

In non-government cemeteries, the family is responsible for covering the installation costs. Various styles of markers are provided, and they must conform to existing monuments. Niche markers for remains are also available.

Laugh Matters

A reporter was interviewing a 104 year-old woman: “And what do you think is the best thing about being 104?” the reporter asked. She replied... “No peer pressure.”

Public Health Service personnel. If you believe you may be entitled to these benefits, we encourage you to inquire further.

Ineligible Individuals

Individuals who are not eligible for veterans' burial benefits include divorced spouses, adult children, parents, siblings, and other dependents. Also ineligible are individuals with a dishonorable discharge, those convicted of subversive activities, and individuals convicted of capital crimes.

Markers

Memorials are provided at no cost for all veterans, spouses, and dependent children interred in a national cemetery. For veterans who passed away before September 11, 2001, markers are available for their graves—excluding spouses or dependents—unless a private memorial already exists.

For veterans who died on or after September 11, 2001, the government will supply a headstone even if a private marker is already in place. The family is responsible for the installation costs if the burial is in a non-government cemetery. Various styles of markers are offered and must align with existing monuments. Niche markers for remains are also offered.

The inscription must include the name, branch of service, year of birth, and year of death—in that order. It may optionally feature an emblem of belief, rank, and decorations earned. Additional personalization such as nicknames or terms of endearment may be added at the family's expense, subject to approval by the VA.

Additional Benefits and Important Details

Reserving space in a national cemetery is not permitted in advance; arrangements are made only at the time of death. Consequently, there is no assurance that spouses will be buried side-by-side.

Burials in national cemeteries typically do not occur on weekends.

National cemeteries accommodate both traditional body burials and the interment of cremated remains.

Laugh Matters

I've sure gotten old. I've had two by-pass surgeries, a hip replacement, new knees, fought prostate cancer and diabetes, I'm half blind, can't hear anything quieter than a jet engine, take 40 different medications that make me dizzy, winded, and subject to blackouts, have bouts with dementia, have poor circulation, hardly feel my hands and feet anymore, can't remember if I am 85 or 92, have lost all my friends.

But, thank God, I still have my Florida driver's license!

Alert!

The VA has received complaints from veterans who were approached by commercial funeral providers offering free cemetery lots or other supposed veterans' benefits.

These providers are not affiliated with the U.S.

Last Wishes101

DISCOVER PEACE OF MIND

Please inquire with the cemetery about guidelines concerning gravesite decorations beyond natural-cut flowers.

Military or funeral honor guards may be provided by nearby military installations or veterans groups. Fly-overs are reserved exclusively for individuals on active duty at the time of their passing.

Upon request, a flag is provided for the burial of any veteran. Applications should be submitted through the VA and flags can be picked up at a U.S. Post Office. Family members may consider purchasing a flag case from private sources for future display.

Next-of-kin, other relatives, or friends have the option to request a "Presidential Memorial Certificate." Multiple certificates may be requested.

Families have the option to directly apply to the VA for all benefits. While funeral directors may offer to handle this process, it's advisable to inquire about any associated charges for submitting claims.

In cases where the body of a veteran without next-of-kin remains unclaimed from a VA facility and the estate lacks sufficient funds, the VA assumes responsibility for burial costs.

There are no specific casket requirements for routine body burials except for sea burials. If an undertaker is handling the body of an unclaimed veteran, they must provide a more durable alternative to cardboard, unless cremation is planned.

Family members visiting overseas grave sites or memorials can acquire passports without any fees for these visits.

- You can request the National Cemetery System to conduct a search to locate any individual interred in a national cemetery. Along with basic vital statistics, you will need to provide the state where the veteran entered military service.

- There are veterans' cemeteries operated by individual states that may provide comparable benefits, albeit with specific limitations. For a directory of VA cemeteries, check http://cem.va.gov

Laugh Matters

Senior citizens have taken to texting with gusto. They even have their own vocabulary:

BFF: Best Friend Fainted, **BYOT:** Bring Your Own Teeth **CBM:** Covered by Medicare, **FWB:** Friend with Beta-blockers **LMDO:** Laughing My Dentures Out, **GGPBL:** Gotta Go, Pacemaker Battery Low!

An elderly man visited the doctor for a checkup. "Mr. Smith, you're in great shape," said the doctor afterwards. "How do you do it?"
"Well," said Mr. Smith, "I don't drink, I don't smoke, and the good Lord looks out for me. For weeks now, every time I go to the bathroom in the middle of the night, he turns the light on for me." Concerned, the doctor found Mrs. Smith in the waiting room and told her what her husband had said. "I don't think that's anything to worry about," she said. **"And on the bright side, it does explain who's been peeing in the fridge."**

Burial At Sea

Burial At Sea, or the scattering of remains at sea, is available to all veterans and dependents and is provided by the Navy or US Coast Guard. A flag is required, and if supplied by the family—can be returned. If supplied by the Navy, it will not be. Because sea burials are done at the convenience of the military, the family may not witness sea burial.

Bodies intended for sea burial must be embalmed using undiluted embalming fluid to preserve them for at least 60 days. A non-sealing metal casket bound with six nylon bands and weighing an additional 150 lbs. is required.

Twenty-two-inch holes must be drilled in the casket—ten on top, ten on the bottom, and one on each end.

To reach the regional Veterans office in your area, call 800-827-1000.

Laugh Matters

Tell me this won't happen to us!

As a senior citizen drove down the freeway, his car phone rang. Answering, he heard his wife's voice urgently warning him, 'Herman, I just heard on the news that there's a car going the wrong way on Interstate 77. Please be careful!'

'Heck,' said Herman, 'It's not just one car!
It's hundreds of them!

Last Wishes101
DISCOVER PEACE OF MIND

How Social Security Can Help You When A Family Member Dies?

SSA Publication No. 05-10008, ICN 451390, November 2009
It is important to notify Social Security as soon as possible after a person's death. Typically, the funeral director will handle this notification, but you will need to provide them with the deceased's Social Security number to complete the report. If you need to report a death to Social Security yourself, please call our toll-free number or contact your local office. Please note that deaths cannot be reported online. The toll-free number is 1-800-772-1231.

Family members of the deceased may be eligible to receive Social Security benefits if the deceased had worked long enough under Social Security to qualify for benefits. It is important to contact Social Security as soon as possible to ensure that the family receives all the benefits they may be entitled to. Please review the following information carefully to understand the potential benefits available.

A one-time payment of $255 may be provided to the surviving spouse if they were living with the deceased, or if they were receiving specific Social Security benefits based on the deceased's record while living apart. If there is no surviving spouse, the payment will be made to a child who is eligible for benefits based on the deceased's record at the time of death.

Certain family members may qualify for monthly benefits, including:

- A widow or widower age 60 or older (age 50 or older if disabled);
- A widow or widower at any age who is caring for the deceased's child under age 16 or disabled;
- An unmarried child of the deceased who is:
- Younger than age 18 (or up to age 19 if he or she is a full-time student in an elementary or secondary school); or
- Age 18 or older with a disability that began before age 22;
- A stepchild, grandchild, step-grandchild or adopted child under certain circumstances;
- Parents, age 62 or older, who were dependent on the deceased for at least half of their support; and
- A surviving divorced spouse, under certain circumstances.

! Alert!

If the deceased was receiving Social Security benefits, you must return any benefits received for the month of death or any subsequent months. For instance, if the person passed away in July, you must return the benefit received in August. If benefits were deposited directly, contact the bank or financial institution and request that any funds received for the month of death or later be returned to Social Security. If the benefits were issued by check, do not cash any checks received for the month of death or later.

Please return these checks to Social Security as soon as possible.

However, eligible family members may be entitled to receive death benefits for the month in which the beneficiary passed away.

Ordering Death Certificates:

The term "death certificate" can refer to either a document issued by a medical practitioner certifying a person's death or, more commonly, a document issued by an official such as a Registrar of Vital Statistics. This document confirms the date, location, and cause of death as recorded in an official register of deaths.

The details included in a death certificate and the process for obtaining it is governed by each governmental jurisdiction. Each governmental jurisdiction dictates the contents of the Death Certificate and the procedures necessary to legally produce it.

The following procedures are generally applicable across most counties in the United States. For specific regulations governing the issuance of death certificates, you should contact the county where the decedent passed away:

Typically, only individuals who are 18 years of age or older may request a certified copy of a death certificate. To safeguard the confidentiality rights of its citizens, the county may restrict the issuance of certified copies to the following individuals:

- Spouse or immediate family members at least 18 years of age
- Attorneys representing Estates
- Attorneys representing family members
- Attorneys representing persons with a legal interest
- Non-Attorney legal interests/other vital interest
- Third-party private investigators
- Genealogical

To obtain a certified copy of a death certificate, the applicant may need to provide proof of their relationship to the deceased or demonstrate legal interest, along with a valid government-issued photo ID.

The applicant might be required to present one of the following:

- Proof of Relationship, which can be a birth certificate that connects the applicant to the deceased or
- A marriage certificate linking the surviving spouse to the deceased.

For proof of legal interest, acceptable documents might include a will that identifies the deceased and the person with legal interest, an insurance policy, a court order of guardianship, a title to personal or real property listing both the deceased and the applicant as co-owners, or any document that establishes legal interest in the record.

Quick Tip

To obtain a certified copy of a death certificate, the applicant may need to provide proof of their relationship to the deceased or demonstrate a legal interest, along with a valid government-issued photo ID.

Be prepared to present this important identification.

The applicant may need to provide one of the following:

Proof of Relationship:

Examples include a birth certificate that establishes a connection between the applicant and the deceased, or a marriage certificate linking the surviving spouse to the deceased.

Proof of Legal Interest:

Examples include a will connecting the deceased to the person with legal interest, an insurance policy, a court order of guardianship, or a title to personal or real property listing both the deceased and the applicant as co-owners. Any document that establishes a legal interest in the record will also be acceptable.

The applicant must submit a signed application, provide valid government- issued identification or a notarized signature on the application, and pay the applicable fee(s), which can range from no cost to $20.00 per copy.

Please be aware that you may need up to 20 copies of the death certificate.

Alert!

Depending on the deceased's affairs, you may need to provide certified copies of the death certificate to various entities such as banks, credit card companies, mortgage lenders, the IRS, the VA, pension fund administrators, security account managers, and others.

Laugh Matters

When you are young, you want to be the master of your fate and the captain of your soul.

When you are older, you will settle for being the master of your weight and the captain of your bowling team

Last Wishes101
DISCOVER PEACE OF MIND

Shock	Initial shock at hearing the bad news
Denial	Trying to avoid the inevitable
Anger	Outpouring the bottle-up emotion
Bargaining	Looking for a way out
Depression	Final realization of the inevitable
Testing	Seeking realistic solution
Acceptance	Finding way to keep going

What is grief?

Grief is a powerful and often overwhelming emotion, whether it arises from the loss of a loved one or from receiving a terminal diagnosis for oneself or a loved one. Individuals experiencing grief may feel numb and disconnected from daily life, struggling to continue with their usual responsibilities while grappling with their profound sense of loss.

Grief is a natural response to loss and is both a universal and personal experience. The manner in which individuals experience grief can differ significantly and is influenced by the nature of the loss. Examples of such losses include the death of a loved one, the end of a significant relationship, job loss, theft, or the loss of independence due to disability.

Experts recommend that those who are grieving recognize that they cannot control the grieving process and be prepared for the various stages of grief. Understanding the reasons for their suffering can be helpful, as can engaging in conversations with others and addressing issues that contribute to significant emotional pain, such as feelings of guilt related to a loved one's death.

Mourning can persist for months or even years. Typically, the intensity of the pain lessens over time as the bereaved adjust to life without a loved one, come to terms with a terminal diagnosis, or accept the possibility of losing someone they care about.

If you are unsure whether your grieving process is proceeding normally, consult with your healthcare professional. Seeking external support can often be beneficial for individuals trying to recover and adjust to the death of a loved one or a terminal illness diagnosis.

Quick Tip

The most crucial element in recovering from loss is receiving support from others. Even if you are usually uncomfortable discussing your emotions, it is important to express them while grieving.

Sharing your experience of loss can lighten the emotional load. Regardless of where the support originates, embrace it and avoid grieving in isolation. Connecting with others will aid in your healing process.

Overcoming Grief:

After the loss of a loved one, you may go through a period of profound grief. Grief is a natural reaction to loss, reflecting the emotional pain you experience when someone you care about passes away. Although there is no correct or incorrect way to grieve, there are healthy coping strategies that, over time, can help you heal and eventually move forward.

Your grieving process is influenced by various factors, including your personality, coping style, life experiences, faith, and the nature of the loss. Healing takes time and occurs gradually; it cannot be rushed or forced, and there is no standard timetable for grieving. Some individuals may start to feel better within weeks or months, while for others, the process may span years. Regardless of your experience, it is crucial to be patient with yourself and let the process unfold naturally.

It is normal to experience a range of emotions in the early stages of grief, including feelings of insanity, the sensation of being in a bad dream, or questioning your religious beliefs.

- **Shock and disbelief**: Immediately following a loss, accepting the reality of what has happened can be challenging. You might feel numb, struggle to believe that the loss is real, or even deny the truth. If someone you care about has passed away, you may find yourself expecting them to appear, despite knowing they are gone.

- **Sadness**: Profound sadness is perhaps the most commonly experienced symptom of grief. You may experience feelings of emptiness, despair, longing, or deep loneliness. It's also common to cry frequently or feel emotionally unstable.

- **Guilt**: You might experience regret or guilt over things you did or didn't say or do. Feelings of guilt can also arise from certain emotions, such as feeling relieved after a long, difficult illness. Additionally, you may feel guilty for not being able to prevent the death, even if there was nothing more you could have done.

- **Anger**: Even if the loss was not caused by anyone's actions, you may still experience feelings of anger and resentment. If you lost a loved one, you might direct your anger toward yourself, God, the doctors, or even the deceased for leaving you. There may be a strong urge to find someone to blame for the perceived injustice you are facing.

- **Fear:** A significant loss can evoke a range of worries and fears. You might feel anxious, helpless, or insecure, and may even experience panic attacks. The death of a loved one can bring about fears regarding your own mortality, the challenge of living without that person, or the responsibilities you now must handle on your own.

- **Physical symptoms**: While grief is often considered an emotional experience, it frequently manifests as physical issues as well. These can include fatigue, nausea, weakened immunity, changes in weight (either loss or gain), aches and pains, and insomnia.

- **Coping with grief:** The most crucial element in healing from loss is receiving support from others. Even if discussing your feelings is challenging for you under normal circumstances, it is essential to express them while grieving. Sharing your experience can help lighten the burden of grief. Accept support from any source and avoid grieving in isolation. Connecting with others will aid in your healing process.

- **Finding support after a loss:** Rely on Friends and Family, it is the time to lean on those who care about you, even if you typically value your independence and strength. Embrace the support of loved ones rather than avoiding them, and be open to the help they offer. Often, people want to assist but are unsure how; so communicate your needs, whether it's a shoulder to cry on or assistance with funeral arrangements.

- **Draw comfort from your faith:** If you follow a religious tradition, allow its mourning rituals to offer solace. Engaging in spiritual practices that hold personal significance, such as praying, meditating, or attending church, can provide comfort. If you find yourself questioning your faith after the loss, consider speaking with a clergy member or others within your religious community.

- **Join a support group**: Grief can be deeply isolating, even when surrounded by loved ones. Sharing your sorrow with others who have faced similar losses can be beneficial. To locate a bereavement support group in your area, reach out to local hospitals, hospices, funeral homes, and counseling centers.

- **Talk to a therapist or grief counselor:** If your grief feels overwhelming, consider reaching out to a mental health professional who specializes in grief counseling. An experienced therapist can assist you in navigating intense emotions and addressing challenges in your grieving process.

- **Face your feelings:** You may attempt to suppress your grief, but it cannot be avoided indefinitely. To heal, you must confront and acknowledge the pain. Avoiding feelings of sadness and loss only extends the grieving process. Unresolved grief can also result in complications such as depression, anxiety, substance abuse, and health issues.

Quick Tip

Contact a grief counselor or professional therapist if you:

• Feel like life isn't worth living any longer
• Wish you had died with your loved one
• Blame yourself for the loss or for failing to prevent it
• Feel numb and disconnected from others for more than a few weeks
• Are having difficulty trusting others since your loss • Are unable to perform your normal daily activities

Did You Know?

It has been proven that after 21 days most people begin to adjust to the circumstances of a death and start to move on with their lives.

It's important to understand that grief is a personal journey and can fluctuate in intensity.

- **Express your feelings:** You can channel your feelings through tangible or creative expressions. Consider writing about your loss in a journal. If you've lost a loved one, you might write a letter to express things you never had the chance to say, create a scrapbook or photo album to honor their life or engage with a cause or organization that was meaningful to them.

- **Look after your physical health:** The connection between mind and body means that physical well-being often enhances emotional health. To manage stress and fatigue, focus on getting sufficient sleep, maintaining a balanced diet, and engaging in regular exercise. Avoid using alcohol or drugs to mask the pain of grief or to artificially elevate your mood.

- **Don't Let anyone Dictate you:** Don't let others dictate how you should feel, and avoid imposing expectations on yourself as well. Your grief is a personal experience, and only you can determine when it's time to "move on" or "get over it." Allow yourself to experience your emotions without shame or self-judgment. It's perfectly okay to feel anger, to express your frustrations, to cry or not cry. It's also acceptable to laugh, find moments of joy, and let go when you're ready.

- **Plan ahead for grief "triggers:"** Anniversaries, holidays, and significant milestones can stir up memories and emotions. Be ready for an emotional impact, as this reaction is entirely normal. If you're celebrating a holiday or important event with family members, discuss their expectations beforehand and agree on ways to honor the loved one you've lost.

- **When grief doesn't go away:** The sadness of losing a loved one may never fully disappear, but it should not dominate your life. If the pain remains so persistent and overwhelming that it prevents you from moving forward, you might be experiencing a condition known as complicated grief. Complicated grief is akin to being trapped in a prolonged and intense state of mourning. You may struggle to accept the death long after it has happened or become so preoccupied with the deceased that it interferes with your daily activities and affects your other relationships.

Care for the Elderly

This section covers the various facilities and types of care available to senior citizens in most urban areas of the United States.

A retirement home is a multi-residence facility designed for active seniors. Typically, each resident or couple occupies an apartment-style room or suite.

In contrast, retirement villages and retirement communities offer separate, independent homes for active residents, usually for individuals aged 55 and older. While these communities may have Block Watch programs and emergency response options, they do not provide health services. Larger retirement communities, like Sun City, may include hospitals, nursing homes, and other privately or nonprofit-operated facilities.

In-home care is favored for several reasons. A temporary caregiver visits the regular caregiver's home and becomes familiar with the care receiver's routine and environment. This approach allows the caregiver to learn the family's routine, locate medications, and ensure the care receiver remains comfortable in their own home without the stress of transportation and unfamiliar settings. This model can involve friends, family members, or paid professionals.

Day centers often cater to individuals with specific chronic conditions, such as Alzheimer's disease and related dementias, but they may also serve any adult with disabilities. Many centers have a nurse on-site and offer a dedicated space for monitoring vital signs and providing other health services as needed. Additionally, they may provide transportation, personal care, and support groups for caregivers. Medicaid or Medicare may help cover the associated costs.

Therapeutic adult daycare centers provide short-term care for individuals experiencing temporary incapacity due to illness, injury, or recovery from surgery. These facilities offer the advantage of having access to emergency services and professional assistance if needed, and residents may stay for a few days or weeks.

Assisted living residences, also known as assisted living facilities (ALFs), are designed for individuals, typically seniors, who do not require the intensive care provided by nursing homes but seek more companionship and some help with daily activities. The age range of residents can vary by facility. These residences can range from small homes serving a single resident to large facilities accommodating hundreds. Living spaces may include private or semi-private sleeping areas with shared bathrooms, resembling dormitory or hotel-style accommodations. Assisted living facilities typically feature common areas for social activities, along with a central kitchen and dining room where meals are prepared and enjoyed.

Quick Tip

Some assisted living units can be rented monthly like an apartment. Others are bought in perpetuity on the same basis as purchasing a condominium.

Usually, a purchase is made with cash, although in some instances financing is available.

Many facilities agree to repurchase the facility when no longer usable by the occupant paying back up to 80% of its original cost

Laugh Matters

A senior citizen was chatting with his 80-year-old buddy.
"So, I hear you're getting married?" "Yep!"
"Do I know her?"
"Nope!"
"This woman, is she good looking?"
"Not really."
"Is she a good cook?" "Nah, she can't cook too well."
"Does she have lots of money?"
"Nope! Poor as a church mouse."
"Well, then, is she good in bed?"
"I don't know."
"Why in the world do you want to marry her then?"
"Because she can still drive!"

Residents in newer assisted living facilities often have their own private apartments, which are usually self-contained, including a bedroom, bathroom, and sometimes a separate living area or small kitchen. Modern facilities are designed with accessibility in mind, incorporating features such as wheelchair-friendly bathrooms and kitchens, as well as extra-wide hallways and doors to accommodate mobility aids. These facilities are required to fully comply with the Americans with Disabilities Act of 1990 (ADA) or similar local legislation.

Assisted living facilities typically do not have the specialized medical monitoring equipment found in nursing homes, and nursing staff may not be available around the clock. However, trained staff are generally on-site to coordinate necessary medical, health, and dental care services for each resident. Residents usually have the option to select their own medical doctor and dental care providers.

Household chores such as changing sheets, doing laundry, and preparing and serving meals are typically included in the base rent and services of assisted living facilities. Depending on the facility's offerings, additional services may include medication management, assistance with bathing, dressing, toileting, transferring, and insulin injections administered by a registered nurse (RN). Some facilities may even feature an on-site beauty parlor. Grocery services are often available as well. The socialization opportunities provided by assisted living facilities are highly beneficial to residents, as these facilities usually offer a variety of activities tailored to accommodate different disabilities and needs.

Assisted living embodies a philosophy of care and services that fosters independence and dignity. These facilities are regulated and licensed at the state level in the United States. In 2011, the average monthly rate was $3,261.00, reflecting a 2.39% increase from 2010 and a 5.99% rise over the six- year period from 2005 to 2011.

Assisted living units can be rented on a monthly basis, similar to apartments, or purchased outright, akin to condominiums. While most purchases are made with cash, some facilities offer financing options. Many facilities also agree to repurchase the unit when it is no longer needed by the occupant, reimbursing up to 80% of the original purchase price.

Many assisted living facilities also cater to individuals with mental health needs, particularly those with forms of dementia such as Alzheimer's disease, provided they do not pose an imminent risk to themselves or others. In the United States, each state has legislation that specifies not only the level of care required but also the conditions that may be excluded from care in these facilities.

Assisted living residences serve as an intermediate option between living at home and residing in a nursing home. They generally do not offer the continuous skilled nursing care found in nursing homes and hospitals.

Laugh Matters

Two elderly women were out driving in a large car - both could barely see over the dashboard. As they were cruising along, they came to an intersection. The stoplight was red, but they just went on through. The woman in the passenger seat thought to herself, 'I must be losing it. I could have sworn we just went through a red light.'

After a few more minutes, they came to another intersection and the light was red. Again, they went right through. The woman in the passenger seat was almost sure that the light had been red but was really concerned that she was losing it. She was getting nervous.

At the next intersection, sure enough, the light was red and they went on through. So, she turned to the other woman and said, 'Mildred, did you know that we just ran through three red lights in a row? You could have killed us both!'

Mildred turned to her and said, 'Oh, crap, am I driving?'

In contrast, nursing homes, convalescent homes, and skilled nursing facilities provide residential care for individuals who need ongoing nursing support and have considerable challenges with activities of daily living. These facilities typically have nursing aides and skilled nurses available around the clock.

Residents of skilled nursing facilities include both elderly individuals and younger adults with physical or mental disabilities. These facilities often provide physical, occupational, and other rehabilitative therapies following accidents or illnesses. Additionally, some nursing homes offer specialized care for individuals with conditions such as Alzheimer's disease.

An Intermediate Care Facility (ICF) provides healthcare for individuals who are disabled, elderly, or non-acutely ill, typically offering less intensive care compared to hospitals or skilled nursing facilities. These facilities are usually privately funded by the individual or their family, though costs may also be covered by private health insurance or third-party services such as hospice care.

A Skilled Nursing Facility (SNF) is a type of nursing home certified to participate in Medicare, a federal program primarily for individuals aged 65 and older who have contributed to Social Security and Medicare during their working years. Medicaid, a federal program administered in each state, provides healthcare and related services to individuals below the poverty line. Medicaid eligibility varies by state and may include low-income parents, children (including those covered by State Children's Health Insurance Programs or SCHIPs), seniors, and people with disabilities.

Nursing homes offer the most comprehensive care outside of a hospital setting, providing custodial care such as assistance with bathing, dressing, and eating, as well as skilled care delivered by registered nurses. Skilled care includes medical monitoring, treatments, and services from specialized professionals like physical, occupational, and respiratory therapists.

The services nursing homes offer vary from facility to facility. Services include:

- Room and board, Monitoring of medication
- Personal care (including dressing, bathing, and toilet assistance)
- 24-hour emergency care, Social and recreational activities

Hospice Care

Originally, the term "hospice" referred to a shelter. Today, it denotes a specialized facility providing comprehensive care for individuals with terminal illnesses. Hospices focus on managing pain and symptoms related to the terminal condition and offer additional supportive services.

Did You Know?

We come into this world with two extraordinary events in our timeline: the day of our birth and the day of our death. These two events should pale in comparison to the many noteworthy events we experience in between. Your legacy lives on only in the hearts and minds of those who survive you.

What you do in life and how you treat others is what determines your legacy.

Last Wishes101

DISCOVER PEACE OF MIND

When faced with a diagnosis of an incurable disease, patients and their families often encounter a range of questions about hospice care. Although end-of-life care options can be complex, it is crucial for patients and caregivers to thoroughly evaluate all available hospice options.

What Questions Should I Know About Hospice Care at Home?

Home-based hospice care is a common option, even for patients requiring extensive physical support. However, it is essential to carefully assess each hospice agency to ensure their services align with your family's specific needs.

Financial Arrangements

Start by consulting the patient's primary care physician to understand the procedure for accessing hospice care in your area. Typically, the primary physician must complete a form confirming that the patient has an incurable illness and is expected to live six months or less. Once this documentation is in place, the hospice agency will take over the care responsibilities.

Inquire with the hospice agency about how benefits will be transferred and whether all services will be covered or if additional charges will apply. Be aware that some private insurance policies limit the number of days covered for hospice care. Contact the financial manager at the hospice agency or a case manager at your insurance company to check if such limitations affect you. If Medicare is the patient's primary insurance, keep in mind that Medicare coverage for hospice care can change frequently. Ensure you have access to an experienced case manager at the hospice agency to help manage any complexities.

Primary Contacts

Inquire about your primary staff contact for in-home hospice care. Typically, a registered nurse supervises this care; and asks about their training and certification. Additionally, ensure you have access to a medical director if necessary.

Remember, a patient does not have to move into a hospice facility to receive hospice care. The hospice care team can deliver services at the patient's home, in a hospital, or at an extended-care facility such as a nursing home.

As a Care Philosophy

The core philosophy of hospice care is to treat the patient comprehensively. This approach includes managing pain related to the terminal illness, addressing the emotional, spiritual, and social needs of both the patient and their family, and supporting individuals in preserving their dignity and autonomy in the final stages of life.

Laugh Matters

Two elderly ladies had been friends for many decades. Over the years, they had shared all kinds of activities and adventures. Lately, their activities had been limited to meeting a few times a week to play cards.

One day, they were playing cards when one looked at the other and said, 'Now don't get mad at me...I know we've been friends for a long time, but I just can't think of your name! I've thought and thought, but I can't remember it. Please tell me what your name is...
Her friend glared at her for at least three minutes, she just stared and glared at her. Finally, she said, 'How soon do you need to know?

Alerts!

To be completely clear, hospice care does not make any attempt to cure an individual that has been diagnosed with a terminal illness.

Patients typically enter hospice when treatment options for their illness have been exhausted, and it's time to focus on terminal care.

What Hospice Doesn't Provide?

To clarify, hospice care does not aim to cure a terminal illness. Patients usually enter hospice when all treatment options for their illness have been exhausted, shifting the focus to end-of-life care. However, patients can still receive medical treatment for unrelated conditions that are not directly related to their terminal illness. Contrary to some misconceptions, hospice care is not designed to hasten death. Assisted suicide is a separate matter and is not part of the hospice care philosophy or plan.

Alert!

Contrary to what some people believe, hospice is not intended to help a patient die sooner than the natural, expected conclusion of the illness

The Decision to Enter Hospice

Deciding to enter hospice care is a challenging decision. The process starts with a consultation with the patient's primary care physician to confirm that all treatment options have been exhausted and that the illness cannot be cured. Once this is established, the patient, their family, and the physician can determine if hospice care is the appropriate next step.

As noted, senior care encompasses a wide range of services and typically requires the expertise of a physician with a specialization in geriatrics to evaluate and determine the appropriate level of care for each individual.

Did You Know?

A November, 2007 survey on family care giving found that care givers are often burdened by high out-of pocket costs in caring for a spouse or parent at home, but almost 60% of the respondents reported an improvement in the quality of their relationship with the person for whom they cared.

By contrast, fewer than 10% said that their relationship got worse during the time they were caregivers.

The survey also found that 30% of family caregivers caring for older individuals are themselves aged 65 or over; another 15% are between the ages of 45 to 54.

Last Wishes101
DISCOVER PEACE OF MIND

Estate Planning

Regardless of your net worth, having a fundamental estate plan is crucial. It guarantees that your family and financial objectives are addressed after your passing. This book, includes forms for a Power of Attorney, a Living Will, and a Last Will and Testament, which may be adequate for most people. However, consulting with an attorney and a CPA is highly recommended. Additionally, it's advisable for you and your spouse to own your home as community property with the right of survivorship and to have your vehicles and bank accounts jointly named.

1. An estate plan consists of several components, including a will, a power of attorney, and a living will or health-care proxy (medical power of attorney). When creating your plan, it's important to be aware of both federal and state laws related to estates.
2. Starting with an inventory of your assets is a wise approach. This inventory should encompass your investments, retirement accounts, insurance policies, as well as any real estate or business interests. Consider three key questions:
   i) Who do you wish to inherit your assets?
   ii) Who should manage your financial affairs in the event of your incapacitation?
   iii) Who would you prefer to make medical decisions on your behalf if you are unable to do so yourself?
3. Everyone should have a will. A will specifies how you want your assets distributed upon your death and is the ideal place to designate guardians for your children. Dying without a will, known as dying "intestate," can lead to additional costs for your heirs and leaves you without control over the distribution of your assets. Even if you have a trust, a will is still necessary to address any assets not included in the trust.

4. Trusts are not exclusively for the wealthy. They are legal instruments that allow you to set conditions on how and when your assets are distributed after your death. Trusts can help minimize estate and gift taxes and enable asset distribution to your heirs without the expense, delays, and public exposure associated with the probate court, which handles the administration of wills. Additionally, some trusts provide enhanced protection for your assets against creditors and legal claims.

5. Talking openly with your heirs about your estate plans can help avoid disputes and confusion. Inheritance can be a sensitive topic, so clearly communicating your intentions can help prevent conflicts after your passing.

6. The federal estate tax exemption—the amount you can leave to heirs without incurring federal tax—varies frequently. In 2012, estates valued at

Quick Tip

You can leave an unlimited amount of money to your spouse without incurring taxes, but this approach may not always be ideal.

By transferring all your assets to your spouse, you forgo using your estate tax exemption and potentially increase the taxable estate of your surviving spouse.

Explore alternative strategies

Laugh Matters

Three old guys were out walking.
First one said, "Windy, isn't it?"
Second one said, "No, it's Thursday!"
Third one said, "So am I. Let's go get a beer!"

Morris, an 82 year-old man, went to the doctor to get a physical. A few days later, th doctor saw Morris walking down the street with a gorgeous young woman on his arm. A couple of days later, the doctor spoke to Morris and said, "You're reall doing great, aren't you?" Morris replied, "Just doing what you said, Doc - 'Get a hot mamma and be cheerful. The doctor said, "I didn't say that. I said, 'You've got a hea murmur - be careful.'"

less than $5 million were exempt from this tax, with amounts exceeding that threshold taxed at a maximum rate of 35%. However, unless Congress intervenes, the exemption level is set to decrease to $1 million in 2013, with the top tax rate rising to 55%.

7. While you can leave an unlimited amount of money to your spouse without incurring taxes, this approach isn't always ideal. By bequeathing all your assets to your spouse, you forego utilizing your estate tax exemption, thereby increasing your spouse's taxable estate. This can result in a higher estate tax burden for your children if your spouse passes the assets on to them. Additionally, this strategy postpones critical decisions regarding asset distribution until after your spouse's death.

8. There are two straightforward methods to make tax-free gifts and lower your estate value. You can give up to $13,000 annually to an individual, or $26,000 if you are married and the gift is to your spouse. Additionally, you can pay an unlimited amount for someone's medical or educational expenses directly to the institutions providing the services, without incurring gift tax.

9. There are ways to make charitable gifts that offer lasting benefits. By contributing to a charitable gift fund or community foundation, your investment can grow tax-free, and you can designate which charities receive donations both during your lifetime and after your death. We recommend consulting with your CPA or attorney to create an estate plan that aligns with your and your partner's needs

Quick Tip

To obtain certified copies of death certificates you must provide proof of your relationship to the registrant or your legal interest and a valid government-issued picture I.D.

For more on this, refer to the Death Certificate section of this kit

Did You Know?

There are 22,815,000 married households in the U.S. (2010 Census)

52% of the households in the U.S. are headed by persons 55 years of age or older.

55% of all adult Americans do not have a will.

Did You Know?

Avoiding Probate: Many estates have provisions whereby property, autos, bank accounts, etc. are owned jointly by a spouse and ownership passes to the survivor without the need for a probate.

Trusts also allow you to distribute assets to your heirs without the cost, delay, and publicity of probate court.

Last Wishes101
DISCOVER PEACE OF MIND

General Power of Attorney

A power of attorney (POA) is a fundamental legal document that grants an appointed agent the authority to handle a broad spectrum of transactions on behalf of the principal. These responsibilities include managing financial support and care payments, borrowing funds, conducting banking transactions, overseeing property management, handling legal claims, accessing safe deposit boxes, managing insurance and retirement benefits, preparing and filing tax returns, exercising stockholder rights, making gifts, contracting for services, and collecting social security benefits, among other lawful tasks. It's important to note that the authority granted by a POA typically ceases upon the death or incapacitation of the principal, and the principal retains the ability to revoke the POA at any time before then.

Alert!

Notice: These legal documents carry significant legal implications. It is advisable to consult with your attorney to verify their validity and enforceability in your state.

Medical Power of Attorney

This legal form is provided for general informational purposes only. Before using any legal form, it is advisable to have it reviewed by a qualified attorney in your jurisdiction to ensure it meets your specific legal requirements and is valid in your area. If you need further assurance, many local hospitals offer free medical power of attorney forms that have been reviewed for legality in your state. Please refer to the following pages titled "Medical Power of Attorney" to view the forms.

Quick Tip

If you're uncertain about the adequacy of this form, you can often obtain a free medical power of attorney form from a local hospital, which is typically reviewed for legality in your state.

Living Will

A Living Will outlines your preferences for end-of-life care. While the following form should be sufficient for most individuals, it is advisable to consult with an attorney to ensure it meets your specific needs and is legally valid in your jurisdiction.

Trusts

A trust is a legally established arrangement designed to hold ownership of property for the benefit of one or more individuals.

Trusts

Some of the common terms associated with trusts include:

- Grantor: The person creating the trust
- Trustee: Person or institution holding legal title to the property
- Beneficiaries: The people who are intended to benefit from the trust.

What Are Some Common Types Of Trusts?

Trusts come in various types and can be established for different purposes. Some of the most common types include:

Asset Protection Trusts: These are designed to safeguard an individual's assets from future creditor claims.

Charitable Trusts: Created to support a specific charity or the public. These trusts are often used in estate planning to reduce or avoid federal estate and gift taxes.

Implied Trusts: These arise from specific situations where a court concludes that, despite the absence of a formal trust declaration, the property owner intended for the property to be used for a certain purpose or to benefit a particular individual. For instance, if a neighbor asks you to care for her car while she is on vacation and then never returns, this situation creates an implied trust, as she did not intend to give you ownership of the car.

Living or Inter Vivos Trust: Created during the grantor's lifetime. A common type is the revocable living trust, where the grantor transfers property into the trust but retains the right to remove or alter the property as desired. Living trusts can be modified, changed, or revoked during the grantor's lifetime.

Irrevocable Trust: Once established, this type of trust cannot be modified, changed, or revoked, except under exceptional circumstances. Once property is transferred to an irrevocable trust, the grantor cannot reclaim it.

Special Needs Trust: Set up for individuals who are receiving government benefits. An inheritance or gift could jeopardize eligibility for such benefits. This trust allows the beneficiary to enjoy additional luxuries or benefits without affecting their eligibility for government assistance.

Spendthrift Trust: Established to safeguard a beneficiary from selling or pledging their interests in the trust, these trusts protect the assets from the

Quick Tip

Trusts may be created purely for privacy. The terms of a will are public and the terms of a trust are not. In some families, this alone makes the use of trusts ideal. Alternatively, the object of a trust could be a charitable purpose rather than specific beneficiaries.

Laugh Matters

Two elderly couples were enjoying friendly conversation when one of the men asked the other, "Fred, how was the memory clinic you went to last month?"

"Outstanding," Fred replied. "They taught us all the latest techniques and psychological visualization, and association, it made a huge difference for me."

"That's great! What was the name of the clinic?"

Fred went blank. He thought and thought, but couldn't remember. Then a smile broke across his face and he asked, "What do you call that flower with the long stem and thorns?"

"You mean a rose?" "Yes, that's it!" He turned to his wife. . ."Rose, what was the name of that clinic?

beneficiary's creditors. The trust assets remain out of reach until they are distributed to the beneficiary.

Tax By-Pass Trust: Created to allow one spouse to leave money to the other. These limit the amount of federal estate tax that would be payable on the death of the second spouse.

Testamentary Trust: A trust established through a will, which becomes effective only after the death of the testator.

Totten Trust: Established while the grantor is still alive by depositing funds into an account at a financial institution, with the grantor acting as the trustee for another person. This type of revocable trust is structured so that the gift is considered complete only upon the grantor's death or through a clear gift during the grantor's lifetime. The most commonly utilized trust in the United States is the Living Trust.

A Living Trust

A living trust is a flexible trust that the creator, known as the grantor or settlor (according to IRS terminology), can alter or revoke. Living trusts are frequently used because they facilitate the transfer of assets to heirs without the need for probate. This process can reduce costs significantly (since probate fees may be based on a percentage of the deceased's net worth in some states), save time, and ensure privacy (probate records are public, whereas trusts keep asset distribution confidential).

Both living trusts and wills can also be designed to handle unforeseen events, such as incapacity or disability, by granting discretionary powers to the trustee or executor.

The grantor or settlor may also act as a trustee or co-trustee. In cases with multiple co-trustees, the trust document may specify whether each trustee can act independently or if decisions require the consent of all co-trustees. The document may also designate one co-trustee to take over if the grantor becomes incapacitated and cannot continue managing the trust.

There are also some downsides to a living trust in the United States. Beneficiaries do not benefit from reductions in federal estate or state inheritance taxes. Establishing a trust can be costly, with expenses incurred immediately rather than deferred until after the grantor's death. The legal fees for drafting a trust are typically higher than those for creating a will. Additionally, managing a trust can be more expensive over time, as most state laws permit trustees to charge a fee of up to 1% of the estate's gross assets annually for their services.

Probate estate administration fees for a will typically range from 1% of the gross estate for very large estates to 4% for very small estates, and these fees

Quick Tip

Spendthrift Trust:

This is established for a beneficiary in order to protect him or her from selling or pledging away his interests in the trust.

Such trusts are beyond the reach of the beneficiaries' creditors, until such time as the trust property is distributed out of the trust and placed in the hands of the beneficiary.

Laugh Matters

A little old man shuffled slowly into an ice cream parlor and pulled himself slowly, painfully, up onto a stool. After catching his breath, he ordered a banana split.

The waitress asked kindly, "Crushed nuts?"

"No," he replied. "Arthritis."

are charged as a one-time expense rather than annually. The same one-time fees apply if someone dies without a will or a trust (intestate). In such cases, state laws mandate that an intestate probate be initiated at the local courthouse. This process involves identifying, locating, and notifying the decedent's closest relatives, as well as gathering, accounting for, and distributing the decedent's real and personal property to these relatives.

Important protections in probate laws, which safeguard against mismanagement, loss, and embezzlement of a decedent's assets, generally do not apply to trust administration. For estates with a will, probate proceedings are overseen by the probate court. Wills typically require signatures from two to three witnesses, depending on state law. Probate law includes various safeguards, such as bonding requirements for the executor, insurance for real property, monitoring of real estate sales by the executor, and mandatory itemized accountings submitted to the court throughout and at the conclusion of the probate process. These safeguards are absent in trust administration, which is conducted privately unless a conflict arises that necessitates court intervention.

As you can see, trusts can be referred to by various names depending on their specific features or purposes. A single trust may possess multiple characteristics or serve several functions, leading to it being described in several ways. For instance, a living trust might also be classified as an express trust, a revocable trust, and potentially an incentive trust, among other types.

! Alert!

Because of the varied number of trusts and the complications involved, we believe you need an Attorney's Help In Creating A Trust.

Trusts can be structured to handle a variety of situations, but careful drafting is essential to make the plan work. If you choose to create a trust, consult with an attorney experienced in estate planning. The potential tax implications and legal formalities of trust drafting make a lawyer's counsel indispensable.

A lawyer can explain all your options and help you understand what types of trusts are right for you and your family.

Administering Your Estate

This section assumes that you have followed the guidance in this book, prepared a will, and designated the distribution of your assets.

Many documents related to wills refer to the "personal representative," "executor," or "administrator" of your estate. These terms all refer to the same role. This book uses the term "Executor."

Quick Tip

The key qualities that an executor needs are honesty, organization, and communication. Honesty as a virtue speaks for itself. People often overlook, however, the necessity of being organized and the ability to communicate.

The distribution of the will can become a mess if it is handled by someone who simply lacks these key qualities.

Who Should I Appoint?

Generally, you can appoint almost anyone as the executor of your will (with some restrictions noted below). Most wills are fairly simple, and no specialized legal or financial knowledge is usually necessary. Many estates include provisions where property, vehicles, bank accounts, and other assets are jointly owned by a spouse, allowing ownership to transfer to the surviving spouse without probate*. Consequently, the most common choices for executors are spouses, siblings, and children. The main exceptions to this are:

- Children under the age of 18 typically cannot be executors
- Felons typically cannot be executors
- Some states have limitations on out-of-state executors, requiring them to also be primary beneficiaries, so check your state's laws
- Some states require out-of-state executors to obtain a bond to insure the estate against wrongful use, so ensure that whoever you choose can cover such a bond and check your state's laws.

The essential qualities for an executor are honesty, organization, and communication. Honesty is a given, but the importance of being organized and having good communication skills is often underestimated. The distribution of the estate can become chaotic if managed by someone who lacks these crucial attributes.

Each state's laws vary, so it's important to review your state's regulations before naming an executor.

Should My Executor Hire Lawyers or Other Professionals?

While the paperwork required in probate court* doesn't necessitate a legal degree, there are situations where professional help is advisable. If there are disputes, complex property issues, significant tax liabilities, or other complications, an executor should consider hiring a lawyer or, depending on the issue, an accountant. Additionally, executors should not hesitate to seek assistance from the court; if the judge deems it necessary, they will likely recommend obtaining legal counsel

Death and Taxes: Preparing Your Finances for the Inevitable

The saying "nothing is certain but death and taxes" holds a profound truth. While the inevitability of both can seem daunting, preparing your finances can significantly alleviate the burden on your loved ones. Understanding the various taxes that can apply to an estate, such as inheritance and estate taxes, is crucial for effective financial planning. This guide will explore the intersection of death and taxes, providing strategies to minimize tax liabilities and ensure your loved ones' financial security after your passing.

Understanding Estate and Inheritance Taxes

Estate and inheritance taxes can significantly impact the value of the assets your beneficiaries receive. Here's a breakdown of these taxes:

1. **Estate Taxes:** These are levied on the total value of a deceased person's estate before the assets are distributed to the heirs. The federal government imposes estate taxes, and some states have their own estate tax laws.
2. **Inheritance Taxes:** Unlike estate taxes, inheritance taxes are levied on the beneficiaries receiving the assets. The tax rate can vary based on the heir's relationship to the deceased and the amount inherited. Only a few states impose inheritance taxes.

Federal Estate Tax

The federal estate tax applies to estates exceeding a certain threshold, known as the estate tax exemption. As of 2024, the exemption is $12.92 million per individual. Estates valued above this threshold are subject to a tax rate of up to 40%. Strategies to reduce federal estate tax liability include:

1. **Gifting:** Make annual gifts up to the federal gift tax exclusion ($17,000 per recipient in 2024) to reduce the size of your taxable estate.
2. **Charitable Donations:** Leave a portion of your estate to charitable organizations to lower the taxable value.
3. **Irrevocable Trusts:** Transfer assets into irrevocable trusts to remove them from your taxable estate.

State Estate and Inheritance Taxes

State taxes can complicate estate planning, as each state has different laws and exemption limits. Some states have lower thresholds than the federal government, potentially subjecting more estates to taxation. It's crucial to understand your state's specific tax laws and plan accordingly. Consulting with an estate planning attorney familiar with your state's regulations can help you develop effective strategies.

Strategies to Minimize Tax Liabilities

Proper planning can minimize the tax burden on your estate and ensure your loved ones receive the maximum benefit. Here are some strategies:

1. **Lifetime Gifting:** Regularly gifting assets to your beneficiaries can reduce the size of your taxable estate. Use the annual gift tax exclusion and lifetime exemption to your advantage.
2. **Establish Trusts:** Trusts can offer significant tax benefits. Irrevocable trusts, in particular, can remove assets from your taxable estate. Additionally, grantor retained annuity trusts (GRATs) and qualified personal residence trusts (QPRTs) can be effective tools.
3. **Charitable Giving:** Donating to charity can provide income tax deductions and reduce your estate's taxable value. Consider setting up a charitable remainder trust (CRT) or a donor-advised fund.
4. **Life Insurance:** Life insurance proceeds can provide tax-free income to your beneficiaries. Consider an irrevocable life insurance trust (ILIT) to keep the policy's value out of your taxable estate.
5. **Spousal Transfers:** Assets transferred to a surviving spouse are generally exempt from estate taxes due to the unlimited marital deduction. However, be mindful of the potential tax burden on the surviving spouse's estate.

Ensuring Financial Security for Your Loved Ones

Beyond minimizing taxes, it's essential to ensure your loved ones are financially secure after your passing. Here are some key steps:

1. **Create a Comprehensive Estate Plan:** A well-rounded estate plan includes a will, trusts, durable power of attorney, and healthcare directives. This ensures your wishes are carried out and provides clear instructions for your heirs.
2. **Review and Update Beneficiaries:** Regularly review and update beneficiary designations on retirement accounts, life insurance policies, and payable-on-death accounts to ensure they reflect your current wishes.
3. **Communicate Your Plan:** Discuss your estate plan with your family and beneficiaries. Clear communication can prevent misunderstandings and conflicts after your passing.

4. **Document and Organize:** Keep important documents, such as your will, trust agreements, insurance policies, and financial statements, organized and accessible. Inform your executor and trusted family members where to find these documents.
5. **Provide for Liquidity:** Ensure your estate has enough liquid assets to cover expenses such as taxes, debts, and funeral costs. Life insurance policies or a designated savings account can provide necessary liquidity.

Choosing Professional Help

Navigating the complexities of estate and tax planning can be challenging. Working with professionals can provide peace of mind and ensure your plan is effective. Consider the following:

1. **Estate Planning Attorney:** An attorney can help draft legal documents, create trusts, and ensure your estate plan complies with state and federal laws.
2. **Financial Advisor:** A financial advisor can assist with investment strategies, retirement planning, and asset management to maximize your estate's value.
3. **Tax Professional:** A tax professional can provide guidance on minimizing tax liabilities and navigating tax laws.

Preparing your finances for the inevitable intersection of death and taxes is a vital aspect of financial planning. Understanding estate and inheritance taxes, implementing strategies to minimize tax liabilities, and ensuring your loved ones' financial security are crucial steps in this process. By creating a comprehensive estate plan, communicating your wishes, and seeking professional guidance, you can navigate the complexities of death and taxes with confidence, securing your legacy for future generations.

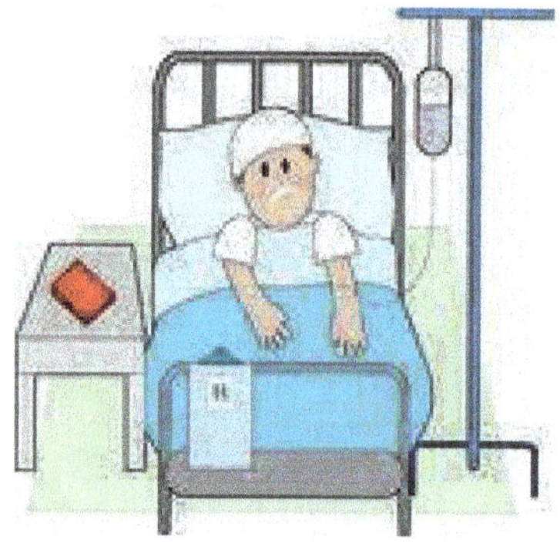

Death with Dignity Act:

The Death with Dignity Act in the USA enables terminally ill patients to request medication to peacefully end their lives. This legislation empowers individuals to make decisions about their end-of-life care, offering them dignity and autonomy during their final days. While there are debates regarding whether this act conflicts with the sanctity of life, proponents view it as a compassionate and humane choice for individuals enduring severe pain and distress.

A primary argument supporting the WITH DIGNITY ACT is that it grants terminally ill patients the choice to end their lives according to their own preferences. For those confronting terminal illnesses, the combination of physical and emotional suffering can become overwhelming, making the ability to decide when and how to end their pain a source of comfort and empowerment. Furthermore, this legislation enables individuals to pass away with dignity, avoiding prolonged and distressing deaths that might not align with their desires.

Opponents of the WITH DIGNITY ACT argue that it undermines the sanctity of life and could lead to abuse or coercion in end-of-life decisions. They believe that permitting individuals to end their lives could set a dangerous precedent and diminish the value of human life. In contrast, supporters of the act contend that it is a personal choice deserving respect, asserting that individuals have the right to make decisions regarding their own bodies and end-of-life care.

The WITH DIGNITY ACT encompasses stringent guidelines and safeguards to ensure that the decision to end one's life is made voluntarily and without external pressure. Patients must be of sound mind and diagnosed with a terminal illness, having a prognosis of six months or less to live. Additionally, they are required to make multiple requests for the medication, undergo consultations with two physicians, and self-administer the medication. These measures are instituted to protect individuals from any potential abuse or coercion.

In conclusion, the WITH DIGNITY ACT in the USA provides terminally ill patients with the option to end their lives with dignity and control. While there are valid concerns regarding the sanctity of life and the potential for abuse, the act incorporates strict guidelines and safeguards to ensure that the decision is made voluntarily and without coercion. Ultimately, this act grants individuals the autonomy to make their own end-of-life decisions and should be respected as a compassionate and humane option for those facing unbearable suffering.

Last Wishes101

DISCOVER PEACE OF MIND

DNR- Do Not Resuscitate (See page 11 for Form)

DO NOT RESUSCITATE

In the United States of America, a DNR (Do Not Resuscitate) order is a legally binding document that communicates to healthcare professionals and emergency responders an individual's decision against receiving cardiopulmonary resuscitation (CPR) during a cardiac or respiratory arrest. This critical document empowers patients to assert control over their medical care and end-of-life preferences. When someone opts for a DNR, they are proactively determining their treatment preferences in life-threatening situations. By clearly outlining these preferences beforehand, individuals ensure that medical providers will honor their wishes. This affords reassurance to patients and their families, knowing that their healthcare decisions will be upheld with respect and dignity.

It is imperative that individuals approach the decision to implement a DNR order with careful consideration and thorough discussion with their loved ones and healthcare providers. Understanding the implications of a DNR order is paramount, as it signifies that certain life-saving measures, such as CPR, will not be initiated in the event of a cardiac or respiratory arrest. Importantly, this choice does not indicate a reduction in the overall level of care provided by healthcare professionals but rather specifies the circumstances under which specific interventions will not be performed.

According to US law, a DNR order must be authorized by a licensed healthcare provider and documented in the patient's medical records. Additionally, individuals can opt to wear a DNR bracelet or necklace, which serves as an alert to emergency responders about their medical preferences. To ensure that their wishes are accurately upheld, individuals should regularly review and update their DNR orders as necessary.

In summary, establishing a DNR order is a critical aspect of advance care planning that empowers individuals to dictate their medical treatment and end-of-life care preferences. By comprehending the ramifications of a DNR order and engaging in discussions with loved ones and healthcare providers, individuals can guarantee that their choices are honored and adhered to. Arizona residents should thoroughly deliberate their decision to implement a DNR order and effectively communicate their intentions to all parties involved in their healthcare.

https://www.azag.gov/sites/default/files/docs/seniors/life-care/2023/b/LCP%20-%20DNR-%20color.pdf

A Do-not-resuscitate (DNR) order is utilized for patients who opt not to undergo resuscitation procedures if their heart or breathing ceases. Typically, this decision applies to individuals in advanced stages of conditions such as cancer or other serious medical ailments. State laws regulate the withholding of resuscitation, often mandating that the patient, along with their primary care physician, notary public, or witnesses, must authorize this form. Signing Requirements- must be authorized by the patient under the state law. Research your state to ensure compliance. **See page 106 for a list of each states' Attorney General's Office email address.**

Contact Information for Each State's Attorney General's Office

State	Email
Alabama	constituentaffairs@ago.alabama.gov
Alaska	attorney.general@alaska.gov
Arizona	AGInfo@azag.gov
Arkansas	oag@ArkansasAG.gov
California	piu@doj.ca.gov
Colorado	cora.request@coag.gov
Connecticut	Attorney.General@ct.gov
Delaware	attorney.general@delaware.gov
Florida	oag.civil.eserve@myfloridalegal.com
Georgia	https://law.georgia.gov/contact-us
Hawaii	hawaiiag@hawaii.gov
Idaho	AGLabrador@ag.idaho.gov
Illinois	attorney_general@atg.state.il.us
Indiana	https://www.in.gov/attorneygeneral/contact-us/general-comments-questions-and-concerns/
Iowa	webteam@ag.iowa.gov
Kansas	https://www.ag.ks.gov/about-us/contact-us/email-us
Kentucky	KyOAGOR@ky.gov
Louisiana	bursar@louisiana.edu
Maine	attorney.general@maine.gov
Maryland	heau@oag.state.md.us
Massachusetts	pamela.spang@mass.gov
Michigan	miag@michigan.gov
Minnesota	attorney.general@ag.state.mn.us
Mississippi	interlocal@ago.ms.gov
Missouri	consumer.help@ago.mo.gov
Montana	governor@mt.gov
Nebraska	ago.info.help@nebraska.gov
Nevada	aginquiries@ag.nv.gov
New Hampshire	attorneygeneral@doj.nh.gov
New Jersey	https://www.njoag.gov/contact/
New Mexico	rtorrez@nmdoj.gov
New York	nysag@ag.ny.gov
North Carolina	jstein@ncdoj.gov
North Dakota	ndag@nd.gov
Ohio	OpinionsRequest@OhioAttorneyGeneral.gov
Oklahoma	contact@oag.ok.gov
Oregon	AttorneyGeneral@doj.oregon.gov
Pennsylvania	info@attorneygeneral.gov
Rhode Island	ag@riag.ri.gov
South Carolina	ODCmail@sccourts.org
South Dakota	consumerhelp@state.sd.us
Tennessee	tnattygen@ag.tn.gov
Texas	disaster-counsel@oag.texas.gov
Utah	https://attorneygeneral.utah.gov/contact/
Vermont	ago.civilrights@vermont.gov
Virginia	https://vaoag.my.site.com/OAG/s/constituent-affairs
Washington	https://fortress.wa.gov/atg/formhandler/ago/ContactForm.aspx
Washington D.C	oagcommunity@dc.gov
West Virginia	communications@wvago.gov
Wisconsin	https://www.doj.state.wi.us/ag/contact
Wyoming	https://attorneygeneral.wyo.gov/contact-us

Last Wishes101
DISCOVER PEACE OF MIND

Leaving a letter to the bereaved

If you found yourself with just one hour left to live, and you could only communicate with your loved ones through a letter, consider it a profound opportunity for self-exploration and a lasting gift to those you cherish. Whether you choose to share it while you're still here or leave it behind for them to read later, this letter could be as concise as a single page or as expansive as a memoir or family history.

Legacy letters often arise during pivotal life transitions like marriage, the birth of a child, or confronting a significant illness. They also emerge when you realize you've lived more life than lies ahead. Through this letter, you have the chance to candidly reflect on your life experiences and core values. You can make sense of your journey, articulate the principles that guided you, and impart the wisdom and lessons you hold dear to future generations.

This letter serves as more than a personal reflection; it provides an opportunity to invigorate yourself and gain new insights into your life. By identifying the values that have shaped you and understanding their origins, you can clarify what truly matters. This is your chance to authentically share how you've lived and ensure that your legacy of values and wisdom endures beyond your lifetime.

Your ethical will or life letter communicates your wishes and sentiments to your loved ones. It includes expressions of affection, blessings, and cherished personal and family narratives, and articulates your core values and desired legacy. You aim to be remembered for these values and hope to impart lasting lessons to your survivors, especially your children and grandchildren. This message can take various forms, such as a concise letter, a compilation of messages, a video recording, or even a published article. According to survey findings by the Financial Planning Association, these "non-financial leave-behinds" hold significantly greater importance for most individuals compared to the financial inheritance from their parents.

Here's an example: Draft a letter to your son, daughter, partner, or sibling, expressing your deep affection and highlighting the cherished memories you've shared together. If you're embarking on a life journey with a loved one or preparing to welcome a child into your life, consider putting down on paper your values, aspirations, concerns, and anticipations. For new parents, it can be an opportunity to
articulate your emotions about the momentous occasion and your dreams for your child's future.

You might take a series of photos from the family album (do it before they're carried off by a hurricane — get a CD made of the best and send copies to the family) and tell stories about what was happening at the time. If your professional work has been especially meaningful, and you have shelves or drawers of documents worth preserving, you might want to spell out to your heirs what you want them to do to preserve your professional legacy. If you want your heirs to support certain causes, here is a chance to explain which ones, and why — and why you led your life the way you did. There are many approaches to writing (speaking, taping) this kind of legacy. -- Pat McNees

Last Wishes101
DISCOVER PEACE OF MIND

let's have DINNER and talk about DEATH

Let's Have Dinner And Talk About Death

Let's dine together and talk about death as an invitation to engage in meaningful conversation whilesharing food. This simple act of dining together can foster a sense of community and strengthen connections with others. By breaking bread and conversing, we have the opportunity to deepen our understanding of each other and strengthen our bonds.

Mealtime provides an ideal setting for exploring a wide range of subjects that spark interesting and insightful discussions. Whether delving into current events, sharing personal stories, or debating differing viewpoints, these conversations allow for thoughtful dialogue. They enable us to broaden our perspectives, embrace new ideas, and cultivate open-mindedness.

Furthermore, sharing a meal and engaging in conversation provides an opportunity to forge deeper connections with others. By dining together, individuals can bond over a shared experience, fosteringlasting memories. Whether with family, friends, or acquaintances, the act of sitting down to eat and converse can strengthen relationships and cultivate a sense of unity.

Additionally, dining and discussing various topics can serve as a form of self-care and relaxation. In today's hectic world, it is crucial to pause, savor a meal, and participate in meaningful dialogue. This simple act allows individuals to unwind and rejuvenate, facilitating genuine connections and nurturing mental and emotional well-being.

In summary, dining together and discussing various topics is a straightforward yet impactful method to build connections and nurture significant relationships. Through sharing a meal and engaging in conversation, we have the opportunity to exchange insights, strengthen bonds, and appreciate moments of relaxation and companionship. Therefore, whenever you gather for a meal, make it a pointto engage in dialogue and genuinely connect with those in your company.

Laugh Matter

Bob, aged 92, and Mary, aged 89, were excited about their decision to get married. While out for a stroll to discuss the wedding, they passed a drug store. Bob suggested they go in.

Bob asked to speak to the pharmacist. He explained they're about to get married, and asked, "Do you sell heart medication?"

"Of course we do," the pharmacist replied.
"Medicine for rheumatism?"
"Definitely," he said. How about Viagra? "Of course."
"Medicine for memory problems, arthritis, jaundice?" "Yes, the works".
"What about vitamins, sleeping pills, Geritol, antacids?" "Absolutely."
"Do you sell wheelchairs and walkers?" All speeds and sizes."
"Good," Bob said to the pharmacist. **"We'd like to register for our wedding gifts here, please."**

Last Wishes101
DISCOVER PEACE OF MIND

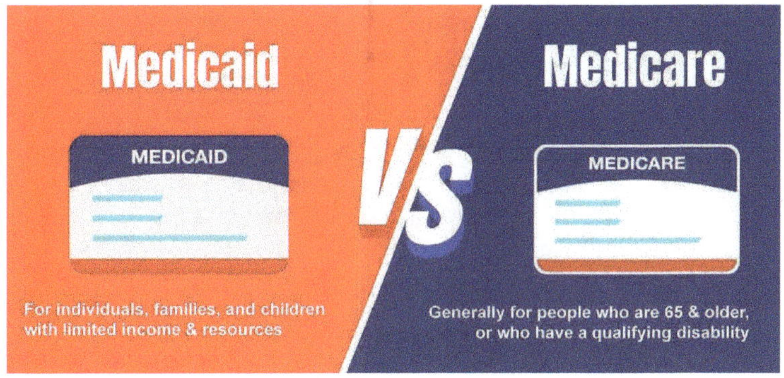

Difference between Medicare and Medicaid.

Medicare and Medicaid are distinct government programs designed to offer healthcare coverage to specific segments of the population in the United States. While both programs share the goal of facilitating access to essential medical services, they differ significantly in their target demographics and funding mechanisms.

One primary distinction between Medicare and Medicaid lies in the populations they serve. Medicare is a federal health insurance initiative primarily intended for individuals aged 65 and older, as well as younger individuals with certain disabilities. In contrast, Medicaid operates as a collaborative effort between federal and state governments, providing healthcare coverage to low-income individuals, families, pregnant women, children, and people with disabilities.

Another notable difference between Medicare and Medicaid pertains to their sources of funding. Medicare is financed entirely by the federal government through contributions from payroll taxes and premiums paid by beneficiaries. In contrast, Medicaid funding is shared between the federal government and individual states, allowing states the flexibility to customize and administer their own programs within federal guidelines.

The coverage options provided by Medicare and Medicaid differ substantially. Medicare is structured into four parts—A, B, C, and D—each addressing distinct healthcare needs such as hospitalization, physician services, prescription medications, and supplemental benefits. Conversely, Medicaid benefits are contingent on state regulations but typically encompass a broad spectrum of medical services including doctor visits, hospital stays, prescription drugs, and long-term care.

Moreover, eligibility criteria for Medicare and Medicaid exhibit notable disparities. Medicare eligibility is primarily based on age—individuals must be 65 years or older—or qualification due to a disability, without regard to income levels. In contrast, Medicaid eligibility hinges on income thresholds and varies among states, with some states extending coverage to individuals with incomes up to 138% of the federal poverty level under provisions of the Affordable Care Act.

In summary, although Medicare and Medicaid both offer healthcare coverage to distinct groups, they differ significantly in the populations they serve, funding mechanisms, coverage offerings, and eligibility criteria. Recognizing these distinctions is crucial for individuals and families navigating access to healthcare services under these governmental initiatives.

Last Wishes101

DISCOVER PEACE OF MIND

Understanding The **Affordable** Care Act (ACA)

ObamaCareFacts.com

Obama Care:

OBAMA CARE EXPLAINED – (Affordable Care Act)

The Affordable Care Act, commonly referred to as Obama Care, was enacted into law by President Barack Obama in 2010. Its primary objective was to ensure accessible and affordable health insurance coverage for all Americans. According to this legislation, individuals are mandated to possess health insurance, failure of which incurs a penalty. This measure aimed to reduce the number of uninsured Americans and enhance the general standard of healthcare nationwide.

One of the primary provisions of the Affordable Care Act, also known as Obama Care, is the establishment of state-based exchanges where individuals can purchase health insurance. These exchanges serve as platforms for comparing various insurance plans and selecting the most suitable option based on individual needs and financial constraints. Furthermore, the law offers subsidies to assist low-income individuals in affording insurance coverage. Additionally, Obama Care expanded Medicaid eligibility criteria to encompass a broader spectrum of low-income individuals and families.

Another pivotal component of the Affordable Care Act, commonly known as Obama Care, is the prohibition of pre-existing condition exclusions. Prior to the enactment of this law, insurance companies had the discretion to deny coverage or impose higher premiums on individuals with pre-existing conditions. Obama Care mandates that insurance providers cannot discriminate against individuals based on pre-existing conditions, thereby ensuring equitable access to affordable health insurance for all Americans.

In addition to enhancing coverage, Obama Care emphasizes preventive healthcare. The legislation requires insurance companies to cover specified preventive services such as vaccinations and screenings without requiring individuals to share the costs. This emphasis on preventive care aims to enhance overall health outcomes and mitigate healthcare expenditures over time.

Despite its numerous provisions and objectives, the Affordable Care Act, has encountered criticism and challenges from diverse quarters. Critics contend that the law imposes excessive regulations on the healthcare sector, potentially encroaching on individual freedoms. Moreover, concerns have been raised about the high costs associated with implementing the law, which some argue places an inequitable burden on taxpayers. Nonetheless, despite these criticisms, Obama Care constitutes a significant stride toward realizing universal healthcare coverage in the United States.

Last Wishes101

DISCOVER PEACE OF MIND

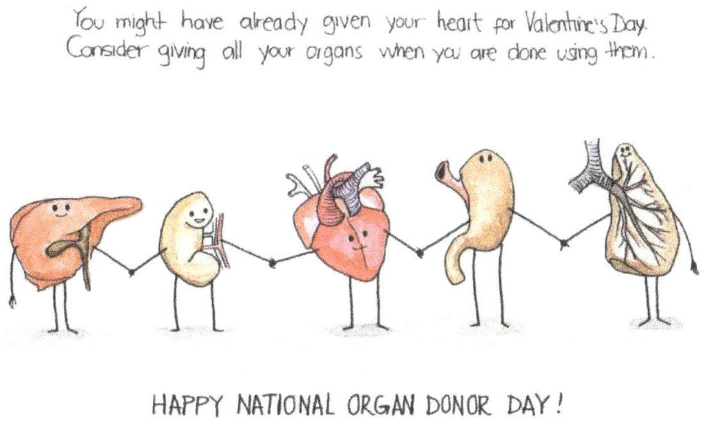

Organ Donations

Organ donations in the United States play a critical role in saving the lives of individuals in urgent need of organ transplants. This process involves individuals generously donating organs such as kidneys or livers, profoundly impacting recipients' quality of life and, in some cases, proving life-saving.

In the United States, the demand for organ donations remains significant due to the large number of individuals awaiting transplants. According to national organizations, there are currently over 2,000 people in the state awaiting life-saving organ transplants. Regrettably, the available supply of organs falls short of meeting this demand, resulting in many individuals not receiving the transplants they urgently require.

The process of becoming an organ donor in the USA is straightforward. Individuals can register as organ donors when renewing their driver's license or by completing an online registration on the designated website. By taking this simple step, individuals can offer hope to those awaiting transplants and potentially save lives in the process.

Organ donations wield transformative power in the USA. By donating an organ, individuals provide others with a second chance at life, enabling them to achieve their fullest potential. The impact of organ donation extends widely, leaving a lasting legacy as recipients and their families are forever grateful for the gift of life.

In conclusion, organ donations in the USA are vital in offering hope and healing to individuals in need of life-saving transplants. Through registration as organ donors, individuals can significantly impact the lives of others and contribute to positive change in the world. It is crucial to raise awareness about the importance of organ donation and encourage others to consider becoming donors. Together, we can save lives and make a meaningful difference in our community.

Last Wishes101
DISCOVER PEACE OF MIND

REVERSE MORTGAGE-

Reverse mortgages represent a financial product available to homeowners in the USA, allowing them to convert a portion convert a portion of their home equity into cash. Unlike conventional mortgages where homeowners repay the lender, in a reverse mortgage scenario, the lender disburses payments to the homeowner. This financial tool is particularly beneficial for elderly individuals facing financial challenges during retirement.

An essential advantage of reverse mortgages is their capability to serve as a supplementary income source for retirees with insufficient retirement savings. By leveraging their home equity, seniors can augment their income to cover essential expenses like healthcare costs, home maintenance, and daily living expenditures. This financial flexibility helps sustain their standard of living and autonomy during their later stages of life.

Another notable benefit of a reverse mortgage is its provision for homeowners to remain in their homes indefinitely. As long as they reside in the property and uphold its upkeep, repayment of the loan is unnecessary. This feature offers reassurance to older individuals who wish to age in place and avoid the complexities associated with downsizing or relocating to a retirement community.

Nevertheless, homeowners in the USA should exercise careful consideration regarding the implications of a reverse mortgage. While it can alleviate immediate financial pressures, it carries potential long-term consequences for their heirs. Upon the homeowner's death or relocation from the property, the loan becomes due and must be settled. This circumstance may impact the inheritance originally intended for their loved ones.

In summary, reverse mortgages represent a significant financial option for elderly homeowners in the United States who seek to enhance their income and maintain residence in their homes. However, it is imperative for individuals to comprehensively grasp the terms and inherent risks associated with these financial instruments before committing. Seeking guidance from a financial advisor or housing counselor can assist homeowners in making a well-informed decision that aligns with their overarching financial objectives.

Last Wishes101
DISCOVER PEACE OF MIND

Guardianships/ Conservatorships

Guardianship and conservatorships are legal mechanisms designed to safeguard individuals who lack the capacity to manage their own affairs. In the United States, these processes are governed by stringent laws and regulations aimed at ensuring the welfare and best interests of the incapacitated person.

Probate, on the other hand, is a legal procedure that addresses the administration and distribution of a deceased individual's estate. In the USA, probate proceedings are typically administered by the probate court in the jurisdiction where the deceased resided. During probate, the court meticulously reviews the deceased person's will, liabilities, and assets, determining the appropriate distribution of assets to their designated beneficiaries.

Guardianship: It is a legal process through which a guardian is appointed to act on behalf of an individual deemed incapacitated. The appointed guardian assumes responsibility for making decisions concerning the person's health, welfare, and financial matters. In the United States, guardianship can be established for minors as well as adults who lack the capacity to make their own decisions due to mental or physical incapacity.

During the guardianship proceedings, the court carefully considers the best interests of the incapacitated person when selecting a guardian to ensure that their needs and welfare are prioritized.

Conservatorship: It is a legal mechanism wherein a conservator is appointed to oversee the financial affairs of an incapacitated individual. In the United States, conservatorships are established when a person is incapable of managing their finances due to incapacity or disability. The conservator assumes responsibility for administering the individual's assets, handling financial obligations such as bill payments, and making financial decisions on their behalf. The court exercises supervision over the conservator's actions to ensure that the individual's financial interests are safeguarded and managed appropriately.

In summary, probate, guardianship, and conservatorship are pivotal legal processes designed to protect individuals who are unable to independently manage their affairs. These processes are governed by specific laws and regulations in the United States to ensure the welfare and best interests of the incapacitated person are upheld. Understanding the roles of probate, guardianship, and conservatorship equips individuals with the knowledge necessary to navigate these legal procedures effectively when the need arises.

Last Wishes101
DISCOVER PEACE OF MIND

Creating Scholarship:

Establishing scholarships in the USA represents a significant avenue for supporting students in realizing their educational aspirations without the financial constraints associated with attending college. Scholarships offer students the chance to pursue their academic ambitions and advance their learning, irrespective of their economic circumstances.

A primary advantage of instituting scholarships in the USA is enhancing accessibility to higher education for students who lack the financial resources to fund college independently. By providing financial aid, scholarships contribute to equalizing opportunities and enabling all students to pursue higher education and fulfill their academic objectives.

Moreover, beyond enhancing accessibility to higher education, scholarships play a crucial role in attracting and retaining top talent within the United States. By awarding scholarships to students who demonstrate academic excellence, leadership qualities, and community engagement, the USA can incentivize talented individuals to remain in the state, thereby fostering economic growth and advancement.

Additionally, establishing scholarships in the United States addresses the pressing issue of student debt. Given the escalating costs of college tuition, many students resort to loans to finance their education. Scholarships offered by the USA mitigate this financial burden, enabling students to graduate without debt and positioning them for future success.

In summary, establishing scholarships in the USA represents a significant investment in the state's future. By offering financial aid to students and enhancing access to higher education, scholarships play a pivotal role in cultivating a more educated and skilled workforce. They also serve to attract top-tier talent to the state and alleviate financial pressures on students. Ultimately, scholarships contribute to ensuring that all students can pursue their academic aspirations and realize their utmost capabilities.

Last Wishes101

DISCOVER PEACE OF MIND

Demystifying Probate: Understanding the Process and How to Navigate It

Probate is often seen as a daunting and complex legal process, but understanding its purpose and the steps involved can help demystify it. Probate is the legal procedure through which a deceased person's estate is administered, ensuring that debts are paid and assets are distributed according to the will or state law if no will exists. This guide will explain what probate is, outline the steps involved, discuss common challenges, and offer tips on avoiding probate through estate planning. Additionally, we'll provide advice on selecting a reliable probate lawyer to help you through the process.

What is Probate?

Probate is a court-supervised process that validates a deceased person's will and oversees the administration of their estate. It involves several key tasks:

1. **Validating the Will:** The court confirms that the will is legally valid.
2. **Appointing an Executor or Administrator:** If the will names an executor, the court officially appoints them. If there is no will, the court appoints an administrator.
3. **Identifying and Inventorying Assets:** The executor identifies, locates, and appraises the deceased person's assets.
4. **Paying Debts and Taxes:** The executor uses estate funds to pay off any outstanding debts and taxes.
5. **Distributing Assets:** After debts and taxes are settled, the remaining assets are distributed to beneficiaries according to the will or state law.

Steps Involved in the Probate Process

The probate process can vary depending on state laws and the complexity of the estate, but generally follows these steps:

1. **Filing a Petition:** The process begins by filing a petition with the probate court to open the estate and validate the will.
2. **Notifying Heirs and Creditors:** The executor must notify potential heirs and creditors of the deceased's passing and the initiation of probate.
3. **Inventorying the Estate:** The executor compiles a comprehensive inventory of the deceased's assets, including real estate, bank accounts, investments, and personal property.
4. **Appraising Assets:** Some assets may require professional appraisal to determine their value.

5. **Paying Debts and Taxes:** The executor settles the deceased's debts and any applicable taxes using estate funds.
6. **Distributing Assets:** Once debts and taxes are paid, the executor distributes the remaining assets to the beneficiaries as outlined in the will or according to state law.
7. **Closing the Estate:** The final step involves filing a petition to close the estate, at which point the court releases the executor from their duties.

Why is Probate Necessary?

Probate serves several important functions:

1. **Legal Validation of the Will:** It ensures that the will is legally valid and accurately reflects the deceased's wishes.
2. **Debt Settlement:** Probate provides a structured process for settling the deceased's debts, ensuring creditors are paid before assets are distributed to beneficiaries.
3. **Asset Distribution:** It ensures that assets are distributed according to the will or state law, providing legal clarity and reducing the potential for disputes.
4. **Protection of Beneficiaries:** Probate offers legal protection to beneficiaries by ensuring the executor fulfills their duties and adheres to the law.

Common Challenges in the Probate Process

The probate process can present several challenges:

1. **Complexity:** Navigating the legal requirements and paperwork can be overwhelming, especially for large or complicated estates.
2. **Time-Consuming:** Probate can be lengthy, often taking several months to years to complete.
3. **Cost:** Probate can be expensive due to court fees, attorney fees, and other administrative costs.
4. **Family Disputes:** Disagreements among beneficiaries or claims against the estate can lead to disputes and delays.

Avoiding Probate Through Estate Planning

Proper estate planning can help you avoid the probate process, saving time, money, and reducing stress for your loved ones. Here are some strategies:

1. **Living Trust:** Creating a revocable living trust allows you to transfer assets to a trust, which are then managed and distributed according to your instructions without going through probate.
2. **Joint Ownership:** Holding property jointly with rights of survivorship ensures that ownership automatically transfers to the surviving owner upon your death.

3. **Beneficiary Designations:** Designating beneficiaries on accounts such as life insurance policies, retirement accounts, and payable-on-death bank accounts allows these assets to bypass probate.
4. **Gifting Assets:** Transferring assets to your beneficiaries as gifts during your lifetime can reduce the size of your estate and avoid probate for those assets.

Selecting a Reliable Probate Lawyer

Choosing the right probate lawyer can make the process smoother and less stressful. Here are some tips:

1. **Experience and Expertise:** Look for a lawyer with extensive experience in probate law and a good track record of handling similar cases.
2. **Reputation:** Seek recommendations from friends, family, or other professionals, and read reviews to gauge the lawyer's reputation.
3. **Communication Skills:** Ensure the lawyer communicates clearly and promptly, explaining complex legal concepts in a way you can understand.
4. **Transparency:** Choose a lawyer who is transparent about their fees and the costs involved in the probate process.
5. **Personal Connection:** It's important to feel comfortable with your lawyer, as probate can be a long and emotional process.

Questions to Ask a Prospective Probate Lawyer:

- How many probate cases have you handled?
- What are your fees and how are they structured?
- What challenges do you foresee in my case?
- How long do you expect the probate process to take for my situation?
- Can you provide references from past clients?

Conclusion

Probate is a crucial process that ensures the proper management and distribution of a deceased person's estate. Understanding the steps involved, the necessity of probate, and how to navigate potential challenges can make the process less daunting. With proactive estate planning, such as setting up trusts and designating beneficiaries, you can minimize the impact of probate on your loved ones. Additionally, selecting a reliable probate lawyer can provide the guidance and support needed to smoothly navigate this legal journey. By taking these steps, you can ensure that your estate is managed according to your wishes, providing peace of mind for you and your family.

12 LIFE LESSONS FROM A MAN WHO HAS SEEN 1200 DEATHS

Deepak Ramola_ May 15, 2016

Rooted in the hearts of many Hindus is the belief that if you breathe your last in Kashi (Varanasi) you attain what is popularly known as 'Kashi Labh' or 'the fruit of Kashi'—moksh or "release from the cycle of rebirth impelled by the law of karma".

Kashi Labh Mukti Bhawan in Varanasi is one of the three guesthouses in the city where people check in to die. The other two are Mumukshu Bhawan and Ganga Labh Bhawan. Established in 1908, Mukti Bhawan is well-known within the city and outside.

Bhairav Nath Shukla has been the Manager of Mukti Bhawan for 44 years. He has seen the rich and the poor take refuge in the guesthouse in their final days as they await death and hope to find peace. Shukla hopes with and for them. He sits on the wooden bench in the courtyard, against the red brick wall and shares with me 12 recurring life lessons from the 12000 deaths he has witnessed in his experience as the manager of Mukti Bhawan:

1. Resolve all conflicts before you go

Shukla recounts the story of Shri Ram Sagar Mishr, a Sanskrit scholar of his times. Mishr was the eldest of six brothers and was closest to the youngest one. Years ago an ugly argument between the two brothers led to a wall to partition the house.

In his final days, Mishr walked to the guesthouse carrying his little paan case and asked to keep room no. 3 reserved for him. He was sure he will pass away on the 16th day from his arrival. On the 14th day he said, "Ask my estranged brother of 40 years to come see me. This bitterness makes my heart heavy. I am anxious to resolve every conflict."

A letter was sent out. On the 16th day when the youngest brother arrived, Mishr held his hand and asked to bring down the wall dividing the house. He asked his brother for forgiveness. Both brothers wept and mid-sentence, Mishr stopped speaking. His face became calm. He was gone in a moment.

Shukla has seen this story replay in many forms over the years. "People carry so much baggage, unnecessarily, all through their life only wanting to drop it at the very end of their journey. The trick lies not in not having conflicts but in resolving them as soon as one can," says Shukla.

2. Simplicity is the truth of life

"People stop eating indulgent food when they know they are going to go. The understanding that dawns on many people in their final days is that they should've lived a simple life. They regret that the most," says Shukla.

A simple life, as he explains, can be attained by spending less. We spend more to accumulate more and thus create more need. To find contentment in less is the secret to having more.

3. Filter out people's bad traits

Shukla maintains that every person has shades of good and bad. But instead of dismissing "bad" people out rightly, we must seek out their good qualities. Harboring bitterness for certain people comes from concentrating on their negatives. If you focus on the good qualities though, you spend that time getting to know them better or, maybe even, loving them.

4. Be willing to seek help from others

To know and do everything by yourself might feel empowering but it limits one from absorbing what others have learnt. Shukla believes we must help others, but more importantly, have the courage to seek help when we're in need.

Every person in the world knows more than us in some respect. And their knowledge can help us, only if we're open to it.

He recounts the incident of an old woman being admitted on a rainy day back in the 80s. The people who got her there left her without filling the inquiry form. A few hours later, the police came to trace the relatives of the old lady who, they said, were runaway Naxalites. Shukla pretended not to know anything. The police left. When the lady's relatives returned next morning, Shukla asked the leader uninhibitedly, "When you can kill 5-8 people yourself why didn't you simply shoot your Nani and cremate her yourself? Why did you make me lie and feel ashamed?" The grandson fell to his knees and pleaded for forgiveness saying no one amongst them is capable of helping his religious grandmother attain salvation. He respects that, and is the reason why he brought her to Mukti Bhawan.

5. Find beauty in simple things

Mukti Bhavan plays soulful bhajans and devotional songs three times a day. "Some people", he says, "stop and admire a note or the sound of the instruments as if they have never heard it before, even if they have. They pause to appreciate it and find beauty in it."

But that's not true of everyone, he adds. People who are too critical or too proud, are the ones who find it hard to find joy in small things because their minds are preoccupied with "seemingly" more important things.

6. Acceptance is liberation

Most people shirk away from accepting what they are going through. This constant denial breeds in them emotions that are highly dangerous. Only once you accept your situation is when you become free to decide what to do about it. Without acceptance you are always in the grey space.

When you are not in denial of a problem you have the strength to find a solution.

Indifference, avoidance, and denial of a certain truth, Shukla believes, cause anxiety; they develop a fear of that thing in the person. Instead, accept the situation so you are free to think what you want to do about it and how. Acceptance will liberate you and empower you.

7. Accepting everyone as the same makes service easier

The secret to Shukla's unfazed dedication and determination towards his demanding job can be understood via this life lesson. He admits that life would've been difficult if he treated people who admit themselves to Mukti Bhavan differently, based on their caste, creed, color, and social or economic status. Categorisation leads to complication and one ends up serving no one well. "The day you treat everyone the same is the day you breathe light and worry less about who might feel offended or not. Make your job easier," he says.

8. If/When you find your purpose, do something about it

To have awareness about one's calling is great, but only if you do something about it.

Last Wishes101
DISCOVER PEACE OF MIND

A lot of people, Shukla says, know their purpose but don't do anything about realising it, making it come to life. Simply sitting on it is worse than not having a calling in the first place. Having a perspective towards your purpose will help you measure the time and effort you need to dedicate to it, while you're caught up in what you think you can't let go or escape. Take action on what truly matters.

9. Habits become values

Shukla recommends cultivating good habits to be able to house good values. And building good habits happens over time, with practice. "It's like building a muscle; you have to keep at it every day."

Till one doesn't consistently work towards being just or kind or truthful or honest or compassionate, every single time he is challenged, one cannot expect to have attained that quality.

10. Choose what you want to learn

In the vastness of the infinite amount of knowledge available to us it is easy to get lost and confused. "The key lesson here is to be mindful of choosing what you deeply feel will be of value to you," he says. People might impose subjects and philosophies on you because it interests them and while you must acknowledge their suggestions, the wise thing to do is delve deeper into what rejoices your own heart and mind.

With a smile on his face Shukla says, "In the last days of their life a lot of people can't speak, walk or communicate with others with as much ease as they could, earlier. So, they turn inwards. And start to remember the things that made their heart sing once, things that they cared to learn more about over the course of their life, which enriches their days now."

11. You don't break ties with people; you break ties with the thought they produce

You can seldom distance yourself from people you have truly loved or connected with in some way. However, in any relationship, along the way, certain mismatch of ideologies causes people to stop communicating. This never means you are no longer associated with that person. It simply means that you don't associate with a dominant thought that person brings with him/her, and to avoid more conflict you move away. The divorce, Shukla affirms, is with the thought and never with the person. To understand that is to unburden yourself from being bitter and revengeful.

12. 10 percent of what you earn should be kept aside for dharma

Dharma, Shukla doesn't define as something religious or spiritual. Instead, he says it is associated more with doing good for others and feeling responsible about that. A simple calculation according to him is to keep 10 percent of your income for goodwill.

Many people donate or do charitable acts towards the end of their life because death is hard on them. In their suffering, they begin to empathize with others' suffering. He says those who have the companionship of loved ones, the blessings of unknown strangers, and an all-encompassing goodwill of people exit peacefully and gracefully. That is possible when you don't cling on to everything you have, and leave some part of it for others.

Project FUEL collects, preserves and passes on life lessons from all across the world. We're currently crowdfunding for our next Masterpiece Tour to Europe, to collect life lessons from refugees displaced after the conflict in Syria. Your contribution counts.

Please go to this link to contribute: https://www.wishberry.in/campaign/collecting-life-lessons-refugees/

ABOUT THE AUTHOR

Deepak Ramola is the Founder and Artistic director of Project FUEL and serves as the indness Ambassador to UNESCO` MGIEP. With his initiative Project FUEL, Deepak travels across the world collecting and passing on life lessons of common people. He is also a gold medalist in ournalism,` an award winning poet, a lyricist and a writer.

Deepak Ramola